MW01120964

Emily's Will Be Done

L. P. Suzanne Atkinson

Produced by:

FriesenPress
Suite 300 – 852 Fort Street
Victoria, BC, Canada V8W 1H8

www.friesenpress.com

Distributed to the trade by The Ingram Book Company

Contents

This book is a penetrating account of the emotional aspects of administering a friend's estate and ensuring that her wishes are fulfilled, despite the frustrations of "red tape". After over forty years as a lawyer in this field, I recommend the book both as a preparation for the layperson who may one day face the same chore, and for the professional who could improve the quality of his services by gaining much insight into the client's point of view.

Borden L. Conrad, Q.C.

This book is an education and a poignant journey of discovery, (and it reads like a guilty pleasure). A must-read for anyone who plans to execute a will, and a should-read for everybody else, Emily's Will Be Done is a striking achievement.

Lynn McCarron

This book is dedicated to David.

I thank David, Wyneth, Pauline, Borden, and Lynn,
as well as that circle of special supporters
(you know who you are)
without whom I could not have ensured
that Emily's Will Be Done

Prologue

A friend and I spend the morning combing through peace-ful roadside graveyards in the sleepy village of Charles River, looking for the grave of Juleen Clarisse Brooks who lived from 1918-1980. I never knew her; only that she was the indulgent mother of my dear friend Emily. Juleen was born in Quebec and buried in Charles River – a minuscule com-munity in the centre of the woods in southwestern Nova Scotia. Emily's Last Will and Testament requests that I scatter a portion of her ashes on her mother's grave. One of my many tasks is to find the grave.

I have a couple of basic scraps of information, specifically her name, date of birth, and date of death. Somehow, back when I searched through the huge three-bedroom traditional house filled to the very rafters with collectibles and the lifetime memories of Emily and her parents, Emily and her husband, and Emily herself (no photo albums, of course), I found a Polaroid picture of Juleen's grave, quite by accident, stuffed in the back of a tattered book about doll collecting. I tucked it away in my ever-expanding manila folder of "this might come in handy" items, part of my struggle with the mountain of possessions, suddenly my sole responsibility.

With this murky picture as my only clue, I called a friend who lives not far from Charles River, and asked for direc-tions to all the graveyards in the area. Without hesitation, she generously offered to give me a personal graveyard tour of her community and on a sunny July 1st morning we met in the parking lot in front of the local general store and set out.

My journey through Emily's life, after her untimely death, brought me many surprises. Emily was an only child of only children. When I met her, both her parents were already dead and she clung to her husband like a drowning fisherman clings to his upturned boat. She talked little of her past; this community never had a place in Emily's life, from what I knew of her. However, the grave shines new light on her family history. A granite-bordered plot frames the graves of her great grandfather, her grandfather and grandmother, and her father and mother. I am stunned. Standing on the side of the hill under an aged and time-worn pine, a carpet of needles beneath my feet; with black flies of summer circling incessantly, I discover Charles River is the seat of her paternal family history. Emily has a story that has never been told.

I am profoundly moved and more than a little saddened that I know virtually nothing about the history of my friend, and now there is no one left from whom I can learn her closely guarded secrets. Charged with scattering ashes in this timeless spot, it is revealed to me that she harboured a special place in her heart for the tiny community tucked into these woods.

I cannot, with any authority, tell you the story of my friend Emily's life. What I will try and tell you is the story of our friendship with its ups and downs, how I managed her affairs, the challenges I faced as I wrapped up her estate, my attempts to respect her wishes, and how I have learned to live with the unanswered questions that will forever haunt me as I wind my way through my own life's journey. I hope to share with you some of the struggles, frustrations, insights, and complications I experienced as an executor, ensuring that Emily's Will Be Done.

Chapter 1
Setting the Stage

When my husband and I decide to buy a rundown Queen Anne revival historic home right on the main drag of what we believe to be one of the most beautiful towns we have ever seen, we have a vision of how our lives will change. Our move to Elmsville, Nova Scotia from northern Alberta comes late in 1991.

In the west, any structure older than twenty-five years would routinely be knocked down to make way for something newer, fresher, and more modern. We fall in love with the Maritime architecture and the lifestyle. Besides, the people are so friendly. We feel we are escaping the north, where we have been running a successful construction business but where the town has suffered a cosmic shift when a huge pulp mill moved in and, in our eyes, ruined the community forever. We pick Nova Scotia to relocate, slow down, start a smaller home renovation business and deal in antiques (my personal passion) out of the house.

So, my goal is to renovate this beautiful century home, have a little antique shop in the front parlour, and support my husband as he limits his vast construction experience to work on hardwood floor and ceramic tile installations. We will downsize and live a simpler life; be closer to my family.

The house has not seen an upgrade of any kind since the 1940s. The smell of mildew, mouse poop and furnace

1

oil assaults me when I walk in the back door. The rooms are huge, the windows big and the staircase can almost speak its welcome. I am in love, and this house loves me back. I run my hand along the old oak banister as I sit on the stairs looking out over the central hall and the country kitchen. This will be home.

Prior to purchasing the property, we completed our due diligence. We talked to the town manager and discovered that Elmsville was not so enthusiastic about an antique shop being established in their little town. We wonder why. Is this not the backbone of Nova Scotia business: catering to the elusive American tourist?

In spite of this, we persevere. We will bring two new businesses to town and restore an old house on the main street into the bargain. We are convinced that we will be an asset to Elmsville; that everybody will see it and appreciate our efforts. We buy the house, apply for the permit, and go back to Alberta to liquidate our business, our property, a piece of land, and as many possessions as we can possibly sell. While still in Alberta, a letter comes from the Town of Elmsville. They are not interested in allowing us a development permit for our little antique business. Apparently, a neighbour has taken up a petition against us, suggesting to the locals that we could potentially rezone the house to commercial status and sell to McDonald's.

Still undaunted, we resolve to clear up any misunderstandings when we get back to Elmsville. We soldier on, driving across the country in a twenty-eight foot U-Haul, towing our SUV, and roll into the yard in Elmsville early in November. We meet the neighbours, with whom we will be sharing a driveway, right off the bat, as the top of our truck rips their phone line clear away from their house. He is a minister and, thankfully, very forgiving.

Without Town permission to open the antique shop, we are determined to worm our way into the hearts of the local business people. We decide to ignore the petition, as well as the fact that the town's primary insurance agent has refused to insure our house citing misrepresentation of our intention to open a commercial operation. Instead of sulking, we join the Elmsville Board of Trade. This will be our way to introduce ourselves to the local movers and shakers. Once they get to know us – and Maritimers are so friendly, after all – there will be no problem. They will be thrilled to have us join their community.

The Board of Trade meeting is held in the Community Centre located in the middle of town. This one is a luncheon catered by the local seniors' group. Entering the room precisely on time, we see the members seated at a very long, narrow table; so narrow that the knees of a person on one side are touching the knees of the person seated opposite. About a dozen men and women occupy the majority of the existing seats. Those with their backs to the door turn around. Everyone stares. No one speaks. We expect, perhaps, the chairperson to rise and introduce herself in an attempt to make us welcome. Nothing. Quickly, my husband and I glance at each other and see in an instant, with that eye-to-eye communication only couples share, that we are both horribly uncomfortable. After all these years, I can still conjure up the anxiety and prickly rise in temperature I felt that day.

A couple, separated from the group by two or three places, stands and motions to seats near them. We walk over and sit down. Quiet introductions follow and our friendship with the Maxwells begins. No one else at the table acknowledges or speaks to us during or after the meeting.

A huge blue and white Victorian guest house, also located on the main street about a ten minute walk from us, graces the entrance to the little town of Elmsville. Emily and Rob Maxwell own this guest house: The Elmsville Inn. Both are retired from the military and moved east to be nearer Emily's parents.

When her parents passed away, Emily and Rob invested their retirement savings in a rundown boarding house and magically restored it into a vibrant and successful inn. The Inn has four guest rooms upstairs along with a kitchen and small TV room. There are two bathrooms for the guests to share. In addition to the entrance foyer and reception desk downstairs, there is a small breakfast room in the front of the house, separated from their apartment by imposing original oak pocket doors. Their private accommodation consists of a living room, small kitchen, storage pantry, single bedroom and bath. I was always incredulous at the breakfast creations Emily was able to produce in that tiny kitchen.

After being members of the Board of Trade for more than a year, Emily and Rob are still treated no better than we were at our first meeting. We are all "Come-From-Aways". Exactly who do we think we are, invading their town to start businesses? Do we think they need us for something? Over the years, Emily and I would often joke about how few locals ever became our patrons. The distant relatives might be put up at The Inn during the odd Elmsville wedding. I would have the occasional neighbour come into the antique shop, after I eventually managed to get that development permit, but only if they had company visiting from away. My business success in the town was only realised by becoming a stop on the local tourist route.

Emily and I start to talk on the phone in the afternoons. We are both housebound by our businesses – me, as I wait for the tourist drive-by traffic; Emily, as she waits for reservation calls or drop-in guests. We become friends over the phone on those long, hot summer afternoons when business is slow but going to the beach, as everyone else does, is not an option.

Emily and Rob are complicated people. In many ways, they are like over-grown children, as they regularly indulge one another regardless of the consequences. To describe them is to explore many extremes and many hidden depths.

Rob's family history is somewhat vague to me. I know his parents are dead and he has a niece in Manitoba. They are uniquely estranged, exchanging polite pleasantries on particular occasions but Rob does not discuss her and Emily, in private, has nothing good to say. It is not until after his death that I learn about a family of multiple marriages, step-siblings, foster siblings and deceased siblings. When I meet some members of the family years later at Rob's funeral, their presence does nothing to clear the muddy waters of Rob's murky family history. After all is said and done, I remain none the wiser.

Rob is a man of slight build, fair complexion, and nondescript features. He is an old fashioned gentleman. He never looks grubby or raggedy like my handyman husband does when he is working around the house or in the yard. He always looks well put together in shirts with button down collars and slacks with a distinct press in the front. A veteran of the Canadian Forces, he did tours in Cyprus in the early 1980s. He has that military no-nonsense attitude when it comes to dealing with the public and coworkers at the tire plant where he works, but Rob's true heart is that of a dreamer. He always looks beyond the horizon to a different lifestyle, a different business, something just out of his reach. Emily, whom he loves more than life itself, indulges his fantasies. Rob is a know-it-all. If you are trading cars, he will tell you what to buy. If you are looking at real estate, he knows the best deals and the best spots. If you need to hire a contractor, he knows the perfect person. Ironically, when it comes time for him to make any major purchases or have renovations done, there are always problems. He and Emily never hire anyone to work around The Inn without feeling ripped off when the work is finished. Rob always expects so much and feels he gets so little.

Kind and generous to his friends and those he loves, Rob can go overboard and you're left forcing him to stop helping. One spring we got the perfect storm of much snow, warm temperatures, and rain combined to the point where water seeped steadily up through our basement floor. We wet vacuumed all night and at three o'clock in the morning, I finally called Rob as I knew he had a new, still in the box, submersible pump. He gave me the pump, which saved our basement (and maybe my marriage). But he also came down to dig the hole for the pump, knowing it was not necessary. One does not argue with Rob, and it is always hard to say thank-you or do anything to repay him. He will have none of that.

My little antique shop keeps me busy. It is open almost every day and I sell at seven antique shows each year. Rob dreams about having a shop of his own, too. He often quizzes me for information on how I find my stock and how I determine prices. The Inn has an outbuilding and his vision is to turn it into a shop. He and Emily are avid collectors, accumulating current collectibles. By that, I mean they buy items new; items they expect will quickly increase in value. After Christmas, they go to department stores and buy all the most recent unsold Barbies and Santa collectibles. At the time of her death, Emily has more than a thousand dolls (many in their original boxes), three hundred Santas (from stuffed to ceramic), a hundred and fifty toy trucks, a significant coin collection, a miniature clock collection, a stamp collection, a rabbit collection, a Chalet glass collection, enough cooking paraphernalia to outfit two inns, and a collection of Gothic dragons. Almost everything is relatively new – 1980 or newer – and in the antique and collectible business, these items are definitely on the collectible end of the spectrum. Most are not worth the original purchase price when thinking of resale.

Rob is determined to renovate The Inn's carriage house into a shop and he spends thousands of dollars working on it. He has display cases custom made to house his most prized possessions. They will be locked, of course, so no one will be able to touch anything. The intent is to liquidate all the acquisitions piled in the back room of The Inn, but I suspect trouble if the customer cannot touch the objects. Sadly, in the end, neither he nor Emily can bring themselves to part with more than a handful of their personal pieces, so they begin buying more things to display in their business, which they name "The Must Have It Shop". They also buy items they think are old, asking me afterwards to come down to have a look and give them an idea of what their finds are worth. They pay retail prices, leaving themselves no room for profit; they unknowingly buy reproductions; they try to resell new products purchased at Zellers the year before. In short, things do not go well. I provide as little advice or ideas as possible, even when asked, because, as you might suspect, even though he makes the request, Rob only wants to hear that he is doing it right. He does not want to hear options or alternative ways of running things. I choose to maintain a respectful friendship by being as supportive as I can be, without being critical or comparative; not easy on some days.

So, this is Rob — the dreamer who believes he knows everything; the military man trained to have planning and organizational skills but who does not allow for consequences; the man who will do anything for his friends and truly believes Emily is the most important person in the universe.

Coming up with a clear description of Emily is a challenge. In fact, to me, Emily was many people: the Emily I knew when Rob was alive; the Emily I came to know after he died; and, most surprising, the Emily I discovered after her sudden, untimely death - the person who somehow saw fit to leave me with this life-changing and overwhelming task.

Emily is a very big woman, morbidly obese, in fact. I never ask her weight, but at about five feet tall, I would estimate her at approximately two hundred and sixty pounds most of the time. Emily does not like herself very much. She complains about her wispy hair, her yellowed teeth, and her swollen ankles. She generally dresses in stretch pants, baggy shirts, and orthopaedic sneakers. It is probably not fair to say she never does herself up, because she will when we meet for lunch in Fiddlehead Bay, or when she has a function to attend. I just don't see that side of Emily very much. She has rosacea, a reddening of the skin on the face, and she seeks out all kinds of treatments which never prove particularly effective. She is the queen of the yo-yo diet. There is nothing she has not tried; every fad, every book, and every program to lose weight. She has been through them all. She confides to me how she came to have such difficulties with her weight. While in the military, it was suggested by her bosses that she drop twenty pounds, and Emily, never one to do anything half-heartedly, stopped eating. Coffee and cigarettes for two weeks and she lost ten pounds. She added a little orange juice on week three and lost another ten pounds. On this first foray into the crash diet world, she lost thirty pounds. Then Rob came home from a tour to Cyprus, they celebrated over Christmas, and she put all the weight back on plus extra as is always the case. Emily started this cycle almost thirty years before she died but I know in my heart of hearts it was a factor that contributed significantly in shortening her life.

Emily runs The Inn with efficiency and grace. The food is glorious; they are regularly booked a year in advance for certain occasions, and the place is spotless. She seems to be the soul of efficiency and organization. Rob works shifts at the tire plant and much of his spare time is spent planning and organizing for his little shop as well as managing the finances for The Inn and for them.

Confined within the walls of her home, Emily turns to crafts. She will decide she is going to take up cross stitching, for example, and buy every conceivable tool, book, pattern and material she can lay her hands on. She executes every craft with the precision and style of a person who has spent a lifetime in the performance of this one application. Once she has achieved this level of expertise, she stops. The challenge is gone and she moves on to another. Emily sews, knits, and crochets. She can do needlepoint, cross stitch, and scroll saw art. She is a gourmet cook and she makes her own sushi. She masters one art after another. This is how she fills the void with a husband who works shift work and the long days waiting for guests to arrive at The Inn.

Being retired military like her husband, Emily has very definite ideas about almost every topic. She commands conversations and always appears to know best, whether it is about business management, marriage, or puppy ownership. She knows a little something about everything. She is never intentionally unkind about this, but oftentimes her motherly approach to my issues causes me to pause and filter the information she shares. At one point in our friendship, I was investigated for breast cancer. Now, this was very troubling and in the end turned out to be nothing but scar tissue from an old car accident, but during the nine months that it took to get a definitive explanation for the test results, I poured my heart out to Emily. Emily figured she already had an explanation for my condition, though. She advised that people working under the kind of stress I did, usually get cancer and die. It shocked me deeply, that she could deal with me so coldly. In her way, she meant well, but this experience certainly affected our relationship for some time afterward, and I became more guarded with my secrets and fears.

Due to the shift work and the inherent obligations of running a small business like The Inn, neither Emily nor Rob is particularly involved in the community. Evening meetings are a hassle and volunteer work takes away from the chores necessary at home. Unlike their military life, which they report as being full of parties, friendships, and lots of involvement in the Canadian Forces community, Emily and Rob stick to themselves in Elmsville. They go for drives in their spare time. They look at oceanfront property and dream of the day they will sell The Inn and move to the country. To my knowledge, they are friends with one other couple besides my husband and me. They are, for all intents and purposes, viewed by the community at large as a mystery.

Emily is a feeder. She shows her appreciation, love, and care for someone with food. One Christmas, my parents came from New Brunswick to celebrate the holidays with us and Emily and Rob suggested we come to The Inn for brunch on Boxing Day. Knowing that Christmas was a very private time for them, I was surprised by the invitation. Normally they would buy mountains of toys for each other and jealously guard their holiday time together. I enthusiastically accepted the invitation.

To this day, I find it hard to describe the experience. We arrived at the house at the appointed time and entered via the guest front door instead of through the back door as usual. Emily was very specific that we come to the front. When they answered the door, they were terribly formal, like actors in a play instead of friends welcoming friends for brunch. Unlike any other visit to the home of a friend, we did not sit together and socialize. We did not help out in the kitchen. We were shown to our seats in the breakfast room of The Inn. Emily worked in the kitchen and Rob served our meal. Everything was so stiff and stuffy. I got up and headed for the sliding doors separating the owners' apartment from The Inn but Rob immediately appeared, blocking my way.

"We will serve you a brunch, today," he said. "Your place is in the breakfast room, Suzanne." I will never forget the baffled look on my father's face. The meal was glorious, of course, beautifully presented and shoulders above anything at restaurants in the area.

After we finished, Emily and Rob came into the breakfast area and sat down for some after-brunch chat. I cannot get over how the conversation unfolded; just what I would imagine their discourse would be with guests during the summer. It was very formal, neutral, and benign. They asked my parents how long they would be staying and about the road conditions on their trip from New Brunswick. They asked David when he would be returning to the job site and what I would do after my parents left town. They stood up together to let us know it was time to take our leave.

This is the only memory I have of an occasion where we gathered together like this. It is much later that I realize Emily prefers not to eat with a group. She and I often share a meal together in later years, but if we are at some sort of function, she never eats. She uses the excuse with others that she is diabetic and can only eat certain things. When I ask her about it, she says a fat person should never eat in public as everyone thinks you are too obese to deserve food. Emily is very hard on herself most of the time.

Chapter 2
Rob's Death and the Aftermath

No one seems to know what the problem is, but Rob has not been well for a couple of years. He loses a lot of time at work and ends up on long-term disability leave. The eventual diagnosis of cancer is vague, certainly as reported to me by Emily. They are not prepared for a terminal diagnosis and try to spin lung cancer into something non-threatening and understandable. It is a horrible time for the two of them. Living more than an hour from treatment, trying to manage their pets and run a business is almost too much for Emily.

By this time, in late 2000, my husband and I have moved across the province to Sunny Point, on the South Shore of Nova Scotia to enable me to take a government job, but Emily and I talk every weekend. She tells me about the doctor's visits, the tests, the treatments (the ones they accept and the ones they do not). When Rob is in the hospital in Halifax, she rides a van shuttle to the city every morning, sits with him all day, and returns on the shuttle at night. It is a huge undertaking and finally she closes The Inn. Rob is dying and Emily fights it as hard as he does. She tells me she feels like his cheerleader; she can never be down or show her true feelings. She saves that for the weekend and for me.

I go to see Rob in Elmsville when he is home. I go to see him in Halifax when he can't get home. I do everything I can to be there for them, trying as gently as I know how, to navigate Emily through those very choppy palliative waters I know full well will end in heartbreak and despair. Emily and Rob have been everything to one another. They say very little to anyone about Rob's condition and no one comes from Manitoba to see Rob or to help Emily.

Deterioration is swift for Rob. The cancer has metastasized to his spine. He is bedridden and then he contracts MRSA. He is just too weak to fight the virus. Emily tells me that, on that last day, she whispered in his ear that it was okay for him to go. She told him she would manage, reassuring him that he could leave her now. He died thirty minutes later.

I note with curiosity that these relatives of vague relationship and status arrive for the funeral en masse. They virtually smother Emily. One evening she calls me, hidden in her bedroom where no one can hear her, to tell me they have filled up every room in The Inn and expect her to wait on them like they are guests. No one even picks up a towel off the floor. They must assume she has staff. She finally decides she will tell them she is able to manage and they can go home. It takes her a week to get The Inn back to rights, although she does not intend to reopen for business. After the dust settles, I go to Elmsville and spend a few days with Emily and "the boys". During Rob's illness, both their small dogs died at different times. Neither one of them could imagine a home without pets so Emily adopted two male kittens. They provide wonderful companionship for Emily after Rob's death and she loves them wholeheartedly.

Neither Emily nor Rob ever gave a thought to having wills, and he has died intestate. She has inherited a fairly substantial estate from Rob, as he passed away before his fiftieth birthday and his insurance payout from the military is huge. They have not insured the mortgage on The Inn but that will be no problem, Emily thinks, because she intends to sell it; she will not even entertain the thought of running it herself. She uses the opportunity of our visit together as a start to explore the options for changes she will make in her life now that she is alone.

The Inn is permanently closed and will be put up for sale. I am shocked to find out that Emily only became an innkeeper to satisfy Rob's dream. She is now anxious to dump the place. She expects to realize a tidy sum and wants the process over as soon as possible. She decides to take up rug hooking, a craft she has always admired but never explored because classes are needed and her lifestyle never permitted this. She wants to join some clubs and get involved in the community for a change. She has decided that when The Inn is sold, she will try and buy a home in a suburb of town, a home she and Rob often admired. The house she has her eye on is huge and about three times the space she needs. It costs a great deal of money, too, but for Emily, this house is the one. She says it is as if Rob is somehow guiding her decision to buy that house. It will be like he is right there with her.

As Emily begins life as a widow, she acts as if Rob is still out there and only delayed from returning for some reason. She treats the whole experience the same way as I imagine she managed his deployments to Cyprus: everything will work out once Rob returns. I try to help without interference, always mindful that my friend is very bright, former military, grieving and trying to fill a bottomless void of loss. I don't feel that I do a very good job most of the time, but trying to balance friendship and counsel is tough. Emily rarely takes my counsel to heart; she asks for advice but proceeds to ignore it, as she and Rob have always done.

Emily has adequate pensions between herself and Rob's legacy, to pay all her bills and live quite comfortably. She does not want RRSP investments; she simply wants her money to be safe and she wants to spend the interest each year on something extra. She asks me what I would do. My suggestion involves secure investments like GICs, laddered so that the interest will pay out annually on some and every two or three years on others – perhaps keep it simple and have a total of five. I also suggest she do some reading and we estimate her interest gains if the money is invested in different ways. Now, I am no financial wizard. I just know where my comfort level is. Emily is not much interested in learning about all this. She goes to the investment arm of her bank and the adviser recommends mutual funds. She takes his advice and invests, unfortunately, just prior to September, 2001. She loses twenty percent almost overnight, as did anyone with money in the stock market, and she is cross – not at herself, but at an investment adviser who suggested a mutual fund would pay her a great return and that she did not have "all that much" to worry about. Asking for my opinion once again, I tell her if it were me, I would move a large chunk of the money out or at least into less volatile mutual funds. She goes back to the adviser who promptly talks her out of it. I never challenge her decisions and she never revisits our discussions. It is as if they never happened.

The sale of The Inn is another uphill battle in Emily's life and another lesson for me as I walk the fine line that allows the support of a friend regardless of their decisions and perhaps, even in spite of their decisions. Emily is desperate to sell The Inn and, as seems always to be the case with real estate, the agents flatter her, build up her expectations and talk about what a wonderful business opportunity it represents. Then they set an exorbitant price tag. The Inn does not sell. Patience is not, and never was, Emily's long suit. She wants the property sold now. She lowers her price and puts an offer on the home she and Rob liked so much. The pressure is on. There is an interested buyer, who does not have adequate funds for the purchase. So, Emily finances the sale herself to the tune of an extra twenty-five thousand dollars as a second mortgage. The buyer agrees to make a payment each month to Emily. I am suspicious. I am just not able to get comfortable with the idea of this buyer's ability to run The Inn and manage to pay both mortgages. Emily and Rob, with all their inherent good will, never did get to the point where they could turn a profit.

The buyer is from Alabama. She has two homes in The States that she has to sell in order to raise sufficient funds to pay for The Inn. She expects to do this "any time now" except that both of her properties need substantial work before they can be put on the market. She has plans to run a pottery shop out of the building Rob used for "The Must Have It Shop". She will run pottery classes as well as manage The Inn. Knowing how hard it is to establish a business in this area, and doubting she has the funds to support three properties, I find all of this impossible to swallow. To top things off, she now buys a piece of land near the centre of the province to raise sheep. I think this woman could perhaps be mentally ill.

Despite my misgivings, Emily refuses to believe what appears obvious to me and soldiers on. There is no other serious interest in The Inn and the closing date for her dream house is fast approaching. You can probably predict how this whole episode ends. The buyer disappears after payments are made to Emily for a mere six months. She moves back to The States and does not respond to attempts by Emily (who hires a private detective) to locate her. The Inn is resold but the new offer does not include repayment of the mortgage owed to Emily. Because she can't afford to sue the original buyer, Emily has to walk away from a debt of almost twenty thousand dollars owed to her. However, she is in her dream home now, and she has no choice but to put this nasty experience in the rear view mirror under lessons learned. The Inn is no longer her responsibility and it is time to look to the future.

In a concerted effort to exercise and lose the weight one last time, Emily sheds almost sixty pounds after the move to her new house. She is bound and determined to get healthy. She buys a new piece of exercise equipment plus a diet and exercise plan from The Shopping Channel. She takes on this new lifestyle as if it will last forever, and I am thrilled to say she looks remarkable and has a new energy and drive. Even though she has only recently joined the local rug hooking guild, in typical Emily fashion, she becomes a renowned rug hooker over the next few years. As with all other crafts, she tackles this task with a vengeance. She attends courses; she buys wool fabric, professional cutters, tools, dyes, and books; she makes beautiful pieces. There is always room to perfect this craft and she never gives it up or gets bored as has happened with everything else. In another burst of energy she also joins the Order of Women's Collective and the Elmsville Food Bank Organization. The new and involved Emily is emerging.

At the same time as all this is happening, she takes on the complete redecoration of the three thousand square foot Cape Cod house she now calls home. Immediately after she moves in, she replaces the kitchen and laundry room floors and hires a custom painter to do all the rooms in the house. Now, this contractor is not your average Joe the Painter, but a designer and her assistant. They glaze, stencil, roll, plastic bag press, scrape, and texture all the walls and ceilings in the place. With the exception of a couple of tables, no furniture has been moved from The Inn, so everything is purchased new. Within the first few months, the master bedroom, kitchen, family room, and all three bathrooms are completely redecorated, including wall removal and bookshelf construction. The master bedroom furniture costs five thousand dollars and the room is painted in Rob's favourite shade of blue. On the dresser sits the urn which contains Rob's ashes. His likeness has been etched into a gold plaque on the side with the engraved words "Love You Forever". In the family room, she has placed two matching recliners and I am struck by the picture she chooses to hang over the fireplace. It's of a couple who dance on an ocean of glass; she is wispy and willowy in a flowing scarlet gown; he is tall and debonair in his tuxedo.

Within two years, Emily has redecorated the house upstairs and down and outfitted the dining room with fabulous furniture, enormously expensive flatware and twelve varieties of crystal stemware — all the trappings for royal get-togethers, yet to my knowledge, no one is to have a meal in that room in the next eight years. It is Emily's showpiece and a memorial to the kind of life she and Rob led when they were in the military and entertained every weekend. Emily has dipped into the insurance money that was decimated by the 2001 stock market crash. I am worried.

The yard is a further venture. Emily is not interested in gardening. She does not like heat, dirt, or bugs. The home, in its original state, was beautifully appointed with hedges, fruit trees, and a great lawn. She hires landscapers who convince her to replace the ten year old brick pavers with redesigned walkways. She has two ornamental shrimp trees placed as sentries on the now curved and cobbled path as it approaches the front door. Just about every original bush and shrub is either pulled up and discarded or moved. She has an exotic rose garden planted, which demands extra attention from the landscapers at least twice a year. She hires someone to weed and someone to mow. The bill for her yard is always double what she expects.

Emily has decided she'd like to start a business selling her collectibles online. The basement is full to the ceiling with collections of dolls, Santas, toys and sundry craft tools of the trade. She buys a computer and a digital camera to take the pictures, accumulating all the necessary equipment to go into Internet sales. She needs help with the technical aspect, as Rob was the one who read instruction manuals and managed technology. He would master an appliance, tool, or gizmo and then show Emily. My husband helps as much as he can, learning how to work the camera, showing her what he's learned and then writing her a cheat sheet for reference when he is not there. He makes a list of the processes required to post an item for sale on Ebay, and then writes her another page of step by step instructions to follow after making a sale. None of it matters. Emily is not compelled to sell. She wants huge prices for everything and the market for online sales has dropped steadily since both 9-11 and Hurricane Katrina. The Canadian dollar is on the rise and this means significantly smaller margins. Americans are just not able to spend as they once did. Emily procrastinates, makes excuses, and laughs about all the stuff she has to do but she would rather rug hook or read a book. In order to make money, you have to be motivated, creative, and hungry. Emily is none of these.

Chapter 3
The Downward Spiral

I see Emily often throughout these years following Rob's death. My job requires travel to the Elmsville area and I often overnight at her home. We enjoy our visits together. We have a little routine where I appear after work, unload the car and prepare to go on a walk with another friend who lives nearby. Emily does not go on walks; she says people always look at the fat girl and think she's investing in a lost cause. She prefers her elliptical and exercises at home. After my walk, Emily and I go for supper. It's usually someplace out of the way and not fancy. Although Emily rarely sees the light of day before eleven a.m., she is always up at the crack of dawn to prepare me a breakfast just like she used to do for guests at The Inn. It does not matter if I protest, she has the pantry full of goodies and she puts on a spread. Most of the time, she even has things arranged for my lunch. If I stay for two nights, she cooks a supper as well. I love these visits; they force me to step away from work while on the road and that does not happen when I stay alone in a hotel. It is during this time, on one of my stays, that she asks me to be her Enduring Power of Attorney and Executor of her will.

Many people get asked to be someone's Enduring Power of Attorney and/or their Executor. My best advice is to understand the importance of clear communication. You will see how important this piece of advice can be, and when I say clear communication, I mean it has to come from both sides. Work experience has prepared me for the responsibilities involved with Power of Attorney issues. I know I will be asked to make decisions on behalf of Emily in the event she is incapacitated in some way, and it will be important to understand exactly what she wants before the time comes. I am confident that I ask all the right questions. Being an executor is another story altogether.

Emily takes on the task of preparing her paperwork for me just like she does everything else. She buys a big filing briefcase, labels everything clearly, shows me where it will be kept for easy access, and says she will always keep the folders up to date with her most recent bank accounts, insurances, mortgage papers, and important documents. Everything is neatly catalogued and in the briefcase so that if anything ever happens to her, I will be able to find her things quickly and efficiently.

Being a bit anal when it comes to record keeping and filing, I am thrilled that Emily has decided to make a will and complete an EPOA. She does not seem as organized as she appeared to be when running The Inn, but she assures me it is her goal to be the epitome of organization in this affair. I can always tell when people are not really serious about this aspiration, as they poke fun at the true organizers, the genetically predisposed methodicals. Emily often teases me about being meticulous. She acts like it is some sort of affliction or character flaw.

I never once inquire about the state of that very important filing briefcase. I never ask if we can go through it again after the first time she shows it to me and brags about how perfectly organized it is. It sits under the desk in the kitchen, in plain sight, collecting dust and cat hair for what turns out to be years. To keep abreast of changes in her financial and personal circumstances would have been wise, but frankly, no matter how strong our friendship, I feel uncomfortable unless Emily brings it up, and she rarely does after the stock market issues. Looking back, I would have discussed in the beginning the idea of reviewing things at least annually, so broaching the subject would have become routine.

Life seems to unfold as expected until sometime in 2006. That summer, Heather, a rug hooking friend of Emily's from out of town, turns up to visit her. My take on this visit comes solely from Emily's reports and my limited interaction with Heather on a few occasions. From what I can gather over numerous telephone calls made when Heather is out of ear shot, something about her presence makes Emily feel inadequate and in many ways, just plain stupid. Heather pokes fun at Emily's dietary choices and says she will waste away having to eat like Emily. Now, I know Emily well enough to know there is lots of non-diet food in the house for Heather. I know she gets a great deal of pleasure in her trips to the grocery store to buy hundreds of dollars worth of supplies so she can prepare sumptuous meals for a guest. Heather, on the other hand, insists that she be fed whatever Emily is eating and then complains about it in some backhanded fashion afterwards.

It seems to Emily as though Heather expects to stay forever. In her reports to me, everything is a drama. Emily does not want Heather's little dog to sleep in the guest room. She does not even let her cats in that room; it is an animal-free sanctuary to accommodate my allergies when I stay there. Furthermore, the dog has frequent accidents in the house. Heather takes the drastic step of sleeping with her dog on the bathroom floor downstairs, even though the dog is perfectly contented in the car overnight. She talks about all the other friends she could be visiting, but makes no plans to leave.

After three weeks, Emily asks me if I will meet them for lunch in Fiddlehead Bay. I have met Heather before, and Emily hopes I can worm a departure date out of her. We get settled in the restaurant and order lunch. Conversation is light and I keep trying to focus on helping Emily, but I cannot get this woman to say anything about end dates, the remainder of her vacation plans, or when she needs to be home. She simply will not reveal a thing. Finally, I come right out with it. "So, Heather, when are you leaving?"

She looks me straight in the face and says, "You know, I haven't given it any thought." Poor Emily's face turns bright red and she orders dessert. After having lost all that weight, this is not typical behaviour for her, and I sense there might be a problem.

Heather finally does leave, but Emily is never quite the same again. I don't know if the visit precipitates the beginning of the end or whether it is mere coincidence, but after the weight starts to come back on, health problems start to turn up one after the other.

As a diabetic, the weight loss had a remarkable effect on Emily. As her weight decreased, her sugars, usually quite unmanageable at the best of times, became controllable. The first thing that happens as she now regains the weight is that she can't keep her sugars under control anymore. She becomes very tired, almost listless, and loses interest in everything around her. The oral medication she is taking doesn't help anymore and she is switched to insulin. To my great relief, the change is remarkable and almost instantaneous. She fully embraces the switch, buying the most up-to-date insulin pens, learning how to read the monitor properly, and researching the most recent literature, all typical Emily. I never understand why she does not lose weight again after this. If she follows the diet her research dictates, one would expect a weight loss. I have no idea what is going on behind closed doors.

It is about a year after Emily starts taking insulin that I get a call from her neighbour, Violet, telling me she has been taken by ambulance from the local clinic to the Regional Hospital. Early reports are that she may have suffered a heart attack. Emily was at the pharmacy and became so short of breath they told her to go to the clinic. She could barely get her car parked, left it in the ambulance bay, and practically fell in the door. Before we know what is happening, she is taken from the Regional Hospital to Halifax and back, with a brand new pacemaker inserted. Her diagnosis is bradycardia. Her heart was beating too slowly and she got very tired.

Again, her energy and attitude improve exponentially. I talk with Emily every week on the phone, sometimes more. I try to pay close attention to her condition by noticing whether her energy seems sapped. When this happens, she provides no details about food bank meetings, the crises within the Order of Women's Collective, or the latest gossip from her rug hooking group. She becomes listless and disinterested in the events of both our lives.

Indeed, Emily starts getting tired again about six months later. She says she can't seem to get out of her own way. Her family doctor, notoriously hard to see, says she is fine and sends Emily to get her pacemaker checked out. No problem. But Emily is short of breath. She starts to sleep sitting up in her lounger instead of going to bed. One wintry afternoon she again ends up in Outpatients at the local hospital. They whisk her to the Regional Hospital by ambulance, admit her, and schedule her to be transported to the city for an examination and angiogram. Apparently, she has had a heart attack. They keep her in the hospital a couple of weeks, and for the first time that she ever admits it to me, Emily is scared. The on call doctor at the Elmsville Outpatient Department told her she could have died while sitting alone at her kitchen table reading her book. Emily tells me she is terrified that she might be dead for days, alone at home, before anyone found her.

After the angiogram, they want to discharge her, but she talks them out of it - no small feat in today's medical system. I offer to go to Elmsville and stay with her until her angioplasty can be scheduled but she will have none of that. It has been a long time since I have had any need to stay at Emily's, and now she seems very determined to keep me from going there. It will only be after her death that I find out why.

Emily finally gets her angioplasty appointment and two stints inserted. Again, she will not let anyone take her to Halifax. She arranges to stay at the Hospital Lodge, has the procedure, and waits a day before driving herself home. Both Violet and I offer to take her and retrieve her, to no avail. Emily fights tooth and nail to maintain her privacy and her independence.

She starts going to the Cardiac Outpatient Clinic taking classes on how to eat properly and how to get back into exercising on a regular basis. This time, I am surprised at Emily's uncharacteristic lack of enthusiasm. I expect her to take this on like all other projects in her life – buy every book, pick up a new piece of exercise equipment, join the local gym, go overboard, but none of this happens. She is quite ho-hum about the whole affair. She rewrites her history a bit to say she didn't have a real heart attack. She has an unusual condition with her arteries. It is not actually heart disease at all. Her cardiologist says so.

The CPAP machine comes next. After repeated attempts to determine why she continues to be so tired, her physician sends her to a sleep clinic. Because of her weight, it is discovered she suffers from sleep apnea and actually stops breathing dozens of times during a night. It is no wonder she feels tired all the time. After she gets the machine, her sleep patterns improve and again, she has more energy.

It is obvious to me that something curious is happening with Emily's health. I cannot put my finger on the problem and I have to admit that I do not ask a lot of direct questions. I let Emily tell me what she wants to tell me. I allow our conversations to go in a direction most often driven by her. She remains involved with some of her major charities but seems to lose total interest in everything else except the two cats. There are no more decorating projects. The front living room remains empty of furniture and unused for ten years except as a storage room for collectibles purchased and never displayed. The cats totally destroy the designer furniture in the family room and there is no discussion about replacing it. Emily has no enthusiasm and is not planning for the future. I worry, but since I want to respect her privacy, that is all I do.

Something is happening with the money, as well. I am not sure what the problem is here, either, but there are indicators difficult to ignore. The first thing is Emily's van. She bought it brand new, loaded, just after Rob died. As you might expect, it does not have high kilometres on it but the warranty has long expired. Every year, Emily talks about getting new and never does. Once she sees the prices of new vans, she gets discouraged. The interest on her investments was initially earmarked for just such purchases but she tells me that she has been pulling money out of those investments each year to pay her landscaping bill (outrageous, in my opinion), her accountant, and her taxes. Emily has no taxes withheld from her pension cheques during the year, saves nothing for taxes owing, and ends up with a huge bill in April. This is how she and Rob always did it and she has no intention of making a change now.

In short, I suspect Emily is having financial problems. Even though I consider us good friends, she never really comes clean about her circumstances; and things are far worse than I suspect. I wish I had asked more questions and risked her becoming cross with me, in order to determine whether there was any way I could have helped. All I did was insist that we both cut back when we exchanged gifts. Emily tended to go overboard, especially at Christmas, and I convinced her we did not need more stuff and one gift plus our traditional lunch in Fiddlehead Bay would be enough holiday celebration. In retrospect, there were little things she could have done to improve her circumstances, but I wonder if she would ever have summoned up the required motivation or self-discipline to get there.

Chapter 4
Getting the Call

Violet and her husband Henry live in a rambling ranch style home next door to Emily. They are wonderful neighbours, not interfering; private people, just like Emily. Over the years, they have looked after each other's cats when someone is away, delivered fruitcake at Christmas, and picked up the mail when the other is sick.

On Thursday, November twelfth, Violet calls me at suppertime to tell me Emily is in the hospital. Violet reports Emily has gone by ambulance to Albertville that morning. She says Emily fainted a few times and decided it was better to call an ambulance than try to drive. Of course, she would never have asked Violet to drive her. I had talked to Emily on Sunday and knew she had a touch of flu. There is a big scare going on about H1N1. People have died and the media hype has become a bit frightening. There are problems with getting flu shots and Emily has not had one. She talked about being achy and short of breath that day, and she had made an appointment with her family physician that couldn't be scheduled until next week.

I call the Regional Hospital after my talk with Violet. Because I am Emily's named next of kin and Enduring Power of Attorney, they let me speak with her even though she is lying in a bed in the Outpatient Department and has not yet been admitted to the floor, as they are short of beds. Here is the story, as she told it to me.

After we talk on Sunday, her condition seems to get worse. By Tuesday, she has a fainting spell in her laundry room. When she regains consciousness on the floor, she discovers she has wet herself. She is weak and wobbly but manages to clean up and spend the rest of the day in her lounger. The next day, she faints again, this time in the hallway immediately after she has descended the steep and slippery polished wood stairs from her second floor. It is a miracle she does not fall down those stairs. I can tell by the whispered tone of her voice that she does not want the hospital staff to hear the details. When she woke this time, she discovers she has wet herself again. Wednesday night, she gets out of bed to go to the bathroom, collapses on the bedroom floor and can't get up. She cannot control her bladder or her bowels and is forced to lie on the floor in her own mess all night, losing consciousness two or three more times. She can't remember how many. In the morning, she manages to haul herself across the room to the other side of the bed and pull the phone down to call the ambulance. To this day, I do not know how she could possibly have managed to clean herself up, get into some clothes, assemble her overnight bag, and pack her CPAP machine. She then calls Violet and asks her to call me. When Violet arrives at the house, she finds Emily perched at the top of the stairs, bedroom door closed, and waiting for the ambulance. She is afraid to descend the stairs and wants the ambulance attendants to assist her. She refuses to let Violet come upstairs or help her to come down. She tells me she could not bear the idea that her neighbour might discover the mess in the bedroom. As is always the case, Emily protects her privacy regardless of the physical cost. Emily divulges all this to me while on the phone in the Emergency Department and still lying in a bed. I tell her I will get someone to cover me at work and be over in the morning, but she insists that she will be okay. She tells me they said she is dehydrated and once she has some fluids on board, they will probably send her home and Violet will come to get her. I tell her okay; I will call in the morning.

I telephone Violet the minute I get off the phone, to get her interpretation of the situation. Violet and Henry take care of Emily's cats whenever necessary, so that concern is resolved. But Violet is still worried. She says something is terribly wrong. Although I know about the incontinence issues, I am anxious to protect Emily's privacy and say nothing about the mess upstairs to her neighbour. Violet simply says the house is in a terrible state and did I think Emily would be upset if she gave her an early Christmas gift and called in the Merry Maids. I tell her I think it would be best if she talk this over with Emily, whom I know would be mortified if the maid service showed up while she was in hospital and discovered the mess in the bedroom.

It's three o'clock in the morning of Friday, November 13, 2009 when I get the call. Don't we all live in fear of that early morning phone call? In the split second between the ring and the answer, I hope against hope it is some disoriented drunk with a wrong number. When David hands the phone across the bed and says it is some Dr. Burrows, he looks confused and a little annoyed but I am instantly alert. I know that Dr. Burrows is Emily's cardiologist, and that something must be very wrong. After the doctor introduces himself, he begins to repeat over and over again that they have done everything they can; that they do not know what has happened. Emily lost consciousness again and they cannot get her back. They tried inserting a tube to assist her to breathe but it was too late. There is nothing they can do and he needs my permission to turn off her pacemaker. His voice shakes, full of tears. He tells me not to drive across the province in the middle of the night; for all intents and purposes, she is gone. She is surrounded by caring nurses and doctors; she will not die alone. He tells me he is glad I have someone with me and I can think over my decision and call him back. He will wait by the phone. He is so sorry, so very sorry.

I do not need to hang up and then call Dr. Burrows back. Thankfully, Emily and I discussed her wishes should something like this happen. As sad and shocking as all this is, I know I can give Dr. Burrows the permission he requires from me to turn off her pacemaker. This could have been the single hardest decision of my life, filled with guilt, remorse, anger, and all kinds of questions. It is the antithesis of all that. In fact, I experience a kind of surreal calm. I know I am well prepared to make the decision that is being put to me. I am in control and able to speak confidently to Dr. Burrows about my discussions with Emily, our friendship, and my complete faith that her wishes will be fulfilled. Emily is not coming back. I grant the permission required to turn off her pacemaker. I do not worry for the next three hours about whether or not I have done the right thing. I spend them in deep reflection about what lies ahead for me, and I have absolutely no clue.

No one ever wants to have to make a decision about "pulling the plug", but if you are required to do so, it's important for your own well-being and state of mind to know the answers to the questions before they are asked. This is one of those situations that will never be forgotten. There are no "do overs", so no matter how difficult and uncomfortable, have the discussion.

I am Emily's executor (executrix, I later learned, is the proper term for the female version). After finding someone to cover my work in the early morning hours of that Friday, we head to Albertville, almost two hours away, to retrieve Emily's things from the hospital and then proceed to Elmsville to find the file box with her important papers. On the way, Dr. Burrows calls to request permission to have an autopsy performed. Poor Dr. Burrows is almost frantic to uncover a cause of death. He feels sure it was not her heart as her pacemaker was in perfect working order. She had a touch of the flu, but that wouldn't kill her. I give my permission, of course, as I feel I have to know, too. Emily was just sixty-two years old. There are too many unanswered questions.

We turn into Emily's driveway. Violet and Henry are instantly beside the car. We are all in shock. There seems to be so much to do and it is not in my nature to admit I do not know where to start. Violet and Henry say they will come in each day to ensure the house is secure and feed the cats. This will satisfy any potential insurance issues. I give the house a cursory glance and my mind races as I see the state of the floors and counter tops in the kitchen. Gently and with knowing and downcast eyes, Violet tells me she has done a walk-through and things are pretty bad upstairs.

I know they are caring people who want to help deal with this tragedy and I trust their integrity and good common sense. Henry will engage Emily's caretaker (who has always ploughed the snow, mowed the grass and done odd jobs for her) to come in and assist him to move carpets and bedclothes out of the house and to the dump. He will help clear the garbage, as well. Henry is physically on the frail side, but mentally, the strongest of us all. Between us we make a plan to clear the decks of cat hair and debris so we can then get to work regarding her clothes, the food, medications and her papers.

I seize the file box from under the desk in the kitchen. Balls of cat hair and dust bunnies roll like tumbleweeds across the floor. I silently wonder how long it has been since she even touched it. I also take her purse and any address books I can find. Her desk is stacked with papers, which I stuff into a tote bag brought with me. I open the drawers and find a cheque register, adding that to my collection. My plan is to retrieve her things from the hospital, speak to the lawyer, and go to the banks. We intended to stay at her house if we needed to, but that idea has changed since our arrival. Because the house is in such a state, we decide we will return home after doing the chores we plan to do.

When I contact the lawyer, he gives me one simple piece of advice. He says that, as executrix, my job is to secure Emily's property and assets. I will need to call the funeral home and make funeral arrangements, but he says that being her executrix and having a copy of her will does not give me access to her bank accounts. We will have to go to Probate Court first. At this point, I do not have a clear idea of what exactly "probate" really is, and I resolve to get better acquainted with the role as soon as possible.

Today, we will talk to the funeral home and get to the hospital. I call Carlson's Funeral Home in Elmsville and speak with Cooper Barnes, the funeral director. We decide to meet the following Monday and he will contact the hospital regarding Emily's body. There will be a delay because of the autopsy and cremation will take place after retrieval from that process. Mr. Barnes is tender, considerate, understanding and helpful. Kindness is very important for me right now. I find I can cope quite well when people share information and answer questions forthrightly. It helps considerably when information is provided to me before I ask for it. You don't know what you don't know.

When I go to the Emergency Department at the Regional Hospital to pick up Emily's belongings, I get the opposite treatment from my experience with Mr. Barnes. Dr. Burrows was very clear on the phone when Emily died. She was surrounded by people who cared, he said; she was not alone. To be fair, there is a shift change around seven o'clock in the morning and anyone involved with Emily the night before would be long gone home to bed, but I still expect, at the very least, some eye contact and maybe a word of sympathy. I wait at the reception desk for some time. When a frazzled little woman snuggled into a blue fuzzy sweater, sporting gold rimmed spectacles perched on the end of her crooked nose, eventually looks up, I finally get to tell my little story about how there was a death last night and I am there to pick up personal effects. Once I explain that my friend died in the Emergency Department, she quickly provides me with directions through the parking lot to the ambulance bay and a vestibule. She then abruptly turns her attention to a lady requesting change for the vending machine. I travel around to the side of the building and patiently wait for someone to appear and attend to my needs. This takes awhile. There are security cameras everywhere and I am obviously not in any distress (at least the kind of distress that would cause bleeding), so it is some time before a person comes through the doors. I have my back to the glass partition, reading a poster about H1N1, when I hear the whoosh of the motor as the automatic doors spring to life. "Can I help you?" I tell my tale. She departs and checks her records, coming back and telling me there is no Emily Maxwell there. I explain again, probably not as calmly as I would have liked, that Emily passed away at three that morning and I am there to pick up her things. Off she goes again, with a bit more arm swinging and a heavier foot than I consider appropriate. She comes back with the black overnight bag and Emily's glasses in her hand. As I peer at the glasses, just loose like that, as if I should just go out to the car and give them to her for the ride home, the collision of circumstances just about puts me over the edge. "What about the CPAP machine?" I ask. Back she goes again, this time with a look of annoyance on her face that could not be mistaken. There is no one waiting in the emergency vestibule, by the way. It does not appear I am preventing anyone from getting medical care, but I certainly feel as if I am doing just that. Back she comes with the CPAP machine. My thank-you and sad little smile of appreciation go unnoticed. There is no sympathy, not even the canned "sorry for your loss" response. I can hardly wait to get out of there.

The Nova Scotia Credit Union in Elmsville is where Emily has her regular chequing account and a couple of savings accounts. No one will see me. I get an appointment for the following Monday morning as I will be in town to meet with the funeral director across the street. The Fundy National Bank in Albertville is where Emily has both her mortgage and her investments. Later on that day, I schedule a meeting with the financial adviser as well as the personal banker. With proof of my executrix status (a copy of the will), they will provide me with statements and information about how we will proceed after probate. I am confident the staff at FNB will be on my side and help me navigate through what I expect to be some very choppy waters. I discover Emily has depleted her investment account significantly since Rob's death and the mortgage, like the one on The Inn, never got insured. It looks like this is going to be a long haul.

I learn fast. Shock and vulnerability influence my perception of the way people treat me. This has a profound effect on my view of the issues thrown my way. No one steps up to assist with decision making. Everywhere I go, from the lawyer to the neighbours, to the banks, to the funeral home, I get the clear message that I am to start the takeover process right now. All the decisions are mine and mine alone. I don't blame anyone for this, although it surprises me that I am expected to jump in and manage Emily's life and death so immediately. No matter how well I know my friend, there are surprises, starting from the moment I walk in the door of her house. I can no longer make assumptions about Emily and her circumstances – just the facts; I will need the facts.

We leave for home, where I spend the next day, Saturday, combing through Emily's personal phone directory, her wallet, and her old address books, trying to contact everyone that seems important to contact. Violet and I have decided that she will call the director of the food bank, the president of the Order of Women's Collective and the leader of the Rug Hooking Guild. They will spread the word. I will deal with all the people mentioned in the will. In no time, I develop the ability to accept assistance, picking a select few people whom I trust. If one of those people offers to do a chore, I let them do it.

The next day and a half is spent making a plan and reviewing all the paperwork I have gathered up when I first entered Emily's home. I come to the realization that the wonderful file box has not been touched in over three years. Any updated documentation is hidden in the rubble I grabbed off her desk, or as I would later discover, in piles all over the house. I make up my mind to treat Emily's estate management like a project at work. I create a ledger and I make lists. I print and plot calendars. I take a week off work. Little do I know! Thank heavens for my tendencies toward detailed documentation and organization that Emily used to find so amusing. I don't yet fully comprehend that all my work will be scrutinized by the court and I will be accountable for every stamp and every kilometre. If you are not organized and able to make a plan, create an expenditure ledger, or deal with lists of lists, then find someone you trust implicitly who is, and employ them to help. The role has the potential to overwhelm even the savviest of organizers.

Chapter 5
No Time to Cry

The nine days that follow Emily's death and drag me steadily to her funeral on November 22 are surreal. I do not keep a diary, which might have been wise, but where would a person ever find the time to examine the moment let alone scratch out the thoughts? Fortunately, I keep calendars where I document occurrences. Timelines are critical every step of the way. I have always functioned better with a plan, but I have no idea how valuable this skill will become in the days ahead. Whenever I review those support documents now, it takes my breath away to recall the volume of tasks accomplished that first week.

After I ensure the cats and house are safely overseen by Violet and Henry next door, I focus on notifications, preparation for probate, Emily's funeral, sale of her van, the collection of numerous copies of her will and death certificate, and notification of the military and her life insurance holder. I only have a week before I return to my work and everything to do with the estate takes place a two hour car ride away.

Somehow, there is no contact information for the beneficiaries in Emily's will. It is not a draft and is now almost ten years old, and I can't help but wonder why her lawyer at the time did not see fit to include addresses. If the lawyer had requested addresses, it probably would have drastically changed the course of executing Emily's will. Half the battle during those first hours is the challenge of initial contact.

Notifications are heart-wrenching, annoying, complicated and exhausting. I have seven people who are mentioned in Emily's will and I start to call as methodically as I can manage, given the circumstances. I identify myself and then tell them that Emily has passed away quite suddenly. I inform them they will hear from her solicitor regarding the contents of her will. I tell them I will be their contact person. It sounds easy enough, but this is not your traditional family and friends scenario. Other than a niece by marriage and the Campbells, both of whom I know, it is a shot in the dark finding people to whom Emily has left bequests. I search her phone books for clues and sometimes find people listed in her personal directory with wrong numbers. On one occasion I called a person who was not the one I sought, but who happened to have a daughter who was friends with the correct person on Facebook. Eventually, I got a call from him.

Each time, it is the same. I heave a sigh as I ask if this is so and so. I identify myself and say I am Emily Maxwell's executrix. I say my call is to inform them that Emily has passed away unexpectedly. Each time I go through this, my throat constricts, my voice shakes a bit more than the last time, my eyes fill with hot tears. I try my best to be clinical, to make the notifications with a clear voice and in concise terms. Some of the people I call are very upset and shocked. This only adds fuel to the fire of these emotions I try desperately to control. Then there are people who need a reminder of who exactly Emily is – the wife of a cousin not seen in years, oh yes, now they remember. Then my grief is pummelled into frustration by people with only a vague recollection of her but wanting to know how much money they will get and when.

I also respond to calls from Emily's friends and colleagues, those from her current community and those from her former military community. As Violet notifies a select few, the word in Elmsville spreads. People are understandably shocked and want to know about the circumstances leading up to Emily's death. I repeat the story many, many times. You would think it would get easier, but it never does.

I have Emily's mail rerouted to me. For a rather substantial fee, the kind folks at Canada Post will readdress mail and forward it along for one year. For the first six months after she dies, Emily gets more mail than I do. She gets craft magazine renewals that require cancellation. She gets bills that are overdue and require payment. She gets catalogues beyond counting. Although I think the readdressing fee from the post office is outrageous, they certainly earn their money when it comes to Emily. At Christmas time, whenever Emily receives a card, and there are many, I try, through Canada 411, to locate the sender and call them to notify them of Emily's death. Needless to say, I am thankful when the mail, and the resulting requirement for notifications, finally stops.

Maybe, if an executor does not know the deceased, the responsibilities carry less emotion. Most executors are connected to the person on some level and a lot of the work, initially, is in the attempt to keep feelings in check while muddling through the necessary tasks required in getting the job done. There is no option to throw your hands in the air and say, "I can't do this."

The two cats become a pathetic problem. Emily's will states clearly that if I cannot find a home to welcome both of her sweet old orange cats – after all, they are eleven years old, brothers, and have always been together - I am to have them euthanized as opposed to splitting them up. Not being able to face the concept of having the boys put down straight away, we put the word out to find new owners for these two spoiled felines. Violet takes over the interim tasks of feeding, watering, and company-keeping. During that first week, many people wish they could take them or think they know someone who might like them, or know someone who wants only one. My husband discovers, quite by chance, the existence of a perpetual cat shelter in a community nearby, run by a veterinarian. All cats are lovingly cared for and housed comfortably, at a very reasonable fee, until they reach old age if a home cannot be found. The day before Emily's funeral, the cats are escorted to the shelter. Although not exactly what

Emily would have expected given her instructions, I execute her wish that they be together in a home and I do not have to cope with the option of euthanasia. As luck would have it, three months later a woman walked into the shelter in search of two mature cats and adopted Tang and Pekoe.

It is profound how much stress a surviving pet can generate for those left behind. Once they were moved to the shelter, Violet shared with me how difficult she found the heartbreaking ritual of caring for these cats every day. Each time she entered the house, she knew they ran to the door in search of Emily, and then retreated swiftly up and away to sit on the refrigerator and silently watch her carry out her daily routine.

The next task at hand is to plan a funeral of some sort. Emily's will is specific about the disposal of her remains, but says nothing about her funeral preferences. Funeral homes and all the trappings can be off-putting to many but I had an exceptional childhood. A school friend was the daughter of an undertaker and we spent many happy hours in the funeral home, tapping out tunes on the organ as we watched Jennifer's father and his assistants wheeling bodies from one part of the building to another. I am quite comfortable in the cool, dimly lit chapels; in the hushed silence of reception rooms with scattered chairs and boxes of tissue placed strategically on tiny side tables. This experience aside, planning someone else's funeral with no guideline of preferences is unfamiliar territory.

Rob's funeral was quite traditional with an open casket, a minister, people speaking, and a big reception. I meet with Cooper Barnes to discuss the arrangements. It is funny how some people are just cut out to be funeral directors. Cooper has all those qualities one might expect. He is soft spoken, respectful, and well versed in the details of death certificates, insurances, options, payments, and reception requirements. He asks all the right questions, provides great suggestions and thoughtfully guides me through the details, and there are a lot. Those who pre-plan their own funeral are wise. It takes a lot of pressure off loved ones, or the executor, if all the details are determined in advance.

Somehow, I know what I want for Emily. It will be a simple celebration of her life and contributions to her community. Cooper suggests, since Emily was not a member of any church, the local Community Church minister might officiate. He will ask and I can set up a time to meet with her. I have already made up my mind that I will not speak at the funeral except for a couple of announcements. It just feels too emotional, somehow, and I have too many things on my plate. The minister, a middle-aged brunette with a no nonsense kind of manner, is kind, asking me to tell her about my friend, and in the end, creating a lovely prologue to the funeral that perfectly suits both Emily and the circumstances.

This particular funeral home consists of a chapel as well as a reception room. Cooper lets me know that I can provide pictures of Emily to display around their reception room and he indicates the Order of Women's Collective, where Emily was member of the executive, has already offered to cater. The inclusion of some examples of her rug hooking might be an option. Emily is renowned in the world of rug hooking, but there are many people in her OWC and food bank circles that might not know that facet of her life. I want representatives from her hooking guild, the OWC, the local food bank, and the Campbell family to speak. I will find willing participants. I will search for pictures, including one that can be used on the front of the service handout. I will gather up examples of her rug hooking. Since an autopsy has been ordered, I have a bit more time than normal and her funeral is scheduled for Sunday afternoon, ten days after her death.

When we return home, I call the presidents of the OWC and the food bank. They both graciously agree to ensure that someone representing their respective organizations will be on hand for the funeral and prepared to speak. Tessa Campbell spoke with eloquence and compassion at Rob's funeral and my request for her to repeat this task for Emily is met with support and sympathy. To think that in less than ten years, she will speak about both of her dear friends in such a way is profoundly sad.

I scour Emily's house for pictures on our next trip to town. During this time, I hear from an old friend of Emily's from Manitoba. Courtesy of some sort of divine intervention, she offers me a lovely picture, taken a couple of summers before, when she visited Emily in Elmsville. She gets her daughter to scan and email the picture and I promptly forward it to Cooper at the funeral home. Yet another task completed. In addition, Meredith asks that her daughter from Halifax be permitted to speak at the funeral in her place. She wants to share a part of Emily's life to which her current friends most certainly have not been privy, but her health circumstances prevent travel. Emily and Meredith were in the military together. They were in training and barracks together. Meredith can tell some great stories. Of course her daughter may participate. We exchange contact information, have a wee cry as we remember our friend and absorb our loss and I, again, let Cooper know the details. The pictures come together finally. Although Emily has no albums, there are photographs and those old fashioned head shots in the cardboard folding frame tucked in the bottom of boxes and dresser drawers. I settle on one of Emily with her parents and their dog, likely taken when Emily was about eighteen, a head shot of Emily when in the military, Emily and Rob's wedding photo and a couple of smaller photos of Emily and Rob at The Inn, later in life.

Emily has done some beautiful rug hooking over the years. I pick out some pieces from her collection, most wrapped in sheets and stuffed in closets, a pillow or two, and a three dimensional wall hanging of what she always referred to as her "silly sheep". There are six little sheep, clustered in a field. Some have spectacles, some have butterflies on their noses and some have funny expressions. It is whimsical and artistic, containing a myriad of complicated and uncommon stitching, all incorporated into the same piece. I will attempt to create a display in the reception room of the funeral home on the day of the service. Another task completed.

Cooper and I are writing the obituary together. I am going through paperwork to ensure I have correct names of her parents, her place of birth, the correct year of her marriage, some information about her military career, and the necessary details about her community activities. I am a believer in memorials – donations to charity in the person's name – not flowers at a funeral, and so I use what I think are the charities from her will as suggestions to potential donors in the obituary. There is the local Pet Care Society and the local Food Bank. The Order of Women's Collective has not been mentioned by Emily, but I include them on the list anyway. When Emily wrote her will, she had not been a member of any groups. I was to get some surprises later on when it came to her charitable bequests.

Sunday is a beautiful late fall day. We drive across the province to Emily's. David has to fix the garburator in the kitchen sink as it has become clogged as we tried to dispose of the contents of the refrigerator. I spend my time prior to the funeral gathering up those things I wish to use in the reception room display. We also plan to return home with her van after the funeral so we can begin the process of cleaning it up to get it ready for sale.

When I arrive at the funeral parlour, I am greeted with a few surprises. As I expect, the chapel is set up and ready to go. Although the notice in the paper specifically says: "in lieu of flowers", Emily's rug hooking friends have ignored this request. Surrounding the box shaped urn that holds her ashes, are eight low, narrow and rectangular glass dishes, each holding about a dozen flowers mounted tightly together. Each arrangement contains a different coloured cluster. Each, they tell me, represents one of the seven friends from her hooking guild and there is a remaining dish to represent me. What is so extraordinary is that the grouping of these flowers around the urn gives the distinct impression of a hooked mat with all the different colours and lineation so characteristic of the craft. It is breathtaking. Another surprise is the program with Emily's picture on the front. It looks beautiful. Emily looks beautiful. Meredith has provided the single nicest picture I have ever seen of Emily and it is perfect.

The turnout is startling. It is huge. The little chapel holds fifty and it fills rapidly. There are representatives from the Order of Women's Collective, the Legion, the Elmsville Food Bank, and her Rug Hooking Guild. There are former guests from the Elmsville Inn and many of her neighbours. I am overwhelmed. I make a few short remarks, thanking people for coming and telling them that the dilemma of Emily's cats has been resolved. I am more emotional than I expected to be and I can feel hot tears puddling up as I gaze out at all the people in the chapel. What surprises me most about the turnout relates to my discussions with the beneficiaries leading up to the funeral. When I told Rob's Manitoba relatives that no one would be able to stay for free in Emily's house (unlike the accommodations provided when Rob died) as I am responsible for keeping the house secure, they decide not to attend. Therefore, my biggest fear was that there would be a pitiful little group sitting in the front row and everything would be over in the blink of an eye. I am so wrong. In my anxiety, I did not factor in the length and breadth of Emily's contacts in her community and the contributions she made.

Emily certainly had impact in the town. I listen to a representative from the Order of Women's Collective, who was also a member of the Rug Hooking Guild, as she stands at the podium barely able to see over the top, wax on about Emily and the work she did for and with them all. I listen to a board member of the food bank. Emily worked tirelessly for these three organizations and gave all she could give. If the truth be known, and it really would not be known until much later, Emily gave of herself to her charities when she had nothing left to give. When at home, she collapsed from exhaustion and did little for herself. Her friend, Tessa, speaks eloquently about her love for the Campbell boys and the spot she holds in the hearts of their family. Meredith's daughter travels from Halifax, sits cuddled against me in the front row, and gets up shyly to speak on behalf of a years old friendship between Emily and her mother. The quiet sounds of giggles and laughter sputter from the group as she talks about life in the barracks and an Emily that no one in that room, including me, ever knew. She tells stories about late nights when they sneak out of quarters; about how Emily taught Meredith to drink and introduced her to the fellas; about a young and popular military clerk who knew everyone and could entertain with the best. It is a simple service to celebrate a life and get to know more pieces of a many layered and multi-faceted Emily. Everyone learns something new that day. My goal is to show the community an Emily they have never known, and instead, they succeed in showing me much the same.

The Order of Women's Collective caters the reception and it looks, from the other side of the room, like pretty slim pickings considering the crowd. They, like me, seemed to have underestimated Emily's influence. This concerns me, but I never get near the table as an endless stream of people approach to talk, thank me, or share their memories of Emily. I am a bit of an oddity and her death remains something of a mystery. "Why me?" "Where was Emily's family?" "What had she died of, anyway?" "Had she been sick?" It is a struggle for me to explain the anticlimactic cause of her death. The autopsy determined she died of a lung infection that progressed undetected and got out of hand. No, it wasn't a heart attack or complications from her diabetes. No one ever said she actually had H1N1 influenza. She had a lung infection; she did not go to the hospital soon enough, obviously, and she died. One woman looks aghast at me and sputters, "This is 2009 not 1899. How can that be?" I don't know.

The reception lasts for what seems like forever. People love the pictures. Of course, many have not been seen by anyone before. They swoon over her hooking projects and want to know what I intend to do with everything and could they buy her wool cutter or her patterns. I spend most of the afternoon gritting my teeth as I try desperately not to tear up when her friends cry openly in front of me. My throat is on fire as I hold back my own unshed grief and attempt to carry on conversations with people I barely know. Constant chatter surrounds me with assaulting voices intending to support and bombarding words intending to comfort.

At one point, two sisters come over to talk to me. They thank me for all the Christmases I have entertained Emily in Sunny Point so she would not have to be alone. Now, Emily never spent Christmas with David and me. Every year, we met for lunch in Fiddlehead Bay shortly before the holiday, as near to Christmas Eve as possible, had lunch, and exchanged gifts, including the cake she always made for David's birthday that falls near the holiday. Emily insisted on spending the big day alone. She wanted it that way. She and Rob had always insulated themselves from the outside world at Christmas and she upheld this tradition to the best of her ability. I respected her wishes and we always talked together on the phone. Initially, I am not quite sure what these women are actually telling me. One Christmas, Emily had dinner with them and their large extended family. I remember her telling me how terribly chaotic it was and how exhausted she was when she finally got home. After that one time, come to find out, Emily always told them she would spend the holiday with me. I smile to myself. This becomes the highlight of my day. I was Emily's excuse to get out of a celebratory event that simply proved too much for her. That's what friends are for.

Chapter 6

It's All About
the Money

Liquidating Emily's vehicle is the first ordeal. We have to sell it, but I am told by her insurance provider I cannot do this until I can present the death certificate and a copy of Emily's will to the Registry of Motor Vehicles and have the title changed from her name into the name of the estate. The insurer must issue a new pink slip. How do I know all this? I don't know anything until I comb through the Internet and call the right people to find out. Every decision is precipitated by a call to someone, a question answered, a protocol clarified.

We bring the van back home, across the province, so my husband can clean it after I go back to work. Poor Emily. I don't think the car has been cleaned in literally years. It takes more than seven hours to restore the inside back to a reasonable facsimile of what a clean van would look like. Before I can sell it, I need a written estimate of its value for probate, and I am cautioned by the lawyer not to sell for less than the estimated value. This is a tall order in the current economy. My role as executor is to realize as much money as possible out of the estate for the beneficiaries. So, we get the written estimate. We get the title changed to the estate. We notify the insurer, and we post the vehicle on Kijiji as soon as possible after the funeral. A couple from Truro come to Sunny Point to have a look, and decide to buy it. By the first weekend in December, the van is sold and the cash is in the bank. This is significant, as I really want to settle the bill for Emily's funeral. Although the will is probated November 24, the bank holding the active accounts takes its own sweet time to process the paperwork that will give me access. There is adequate money to pay her current bills and make her mort-gage payments from her final pension cheques, but I am not able to access her actual bank accounts for the time being. Since I created an estate bank account right after Emily died, I am able to deposit the cash from the vehicle sale, along with those last pension cheques, and start to take financial responsibility on behalf of the estate.

Emily was retired from the Canadian military. The Forces have a particular (meaning not comprehensible to the general public) way of conducting business. My attempts to inform them of her death and access her life insurance become some of the most burdensome tasks of that first month. The military office involved in the acceptance of death certificates and copies of wills is in the process of moving. The contact person for Emily's file is in and out of the office on all kinds of different courses. I am asked to fax the paperwork to another office, as the correct office that was moving does not have their fax set up. Now, they do not lose the paperwork, but it takes seventeen days for the fax to be delivered from the receiving office to the correct person located in another building, and currently off on course. If it sounds like I might have crawled through the phone after someone, you are correct. To top the whole thing off, they want Rob's death certificate as well as Emily's, since Emily was in receipt of a widow's pension. I am thankful that, although Emily did not keep her file box up to date, she was very thorough when she created it. My necessary paperwork is safely stuffed in a folder labelled with Rob's name and military identification.

Every time my husband and I travel to Elmsville, we sort. We go through everything in the house and this is really saying a lot. While we're at it, we have to make preparations to sell her home. We contact our old friend Katie who comes over early in December. This marks the first time we stay there overnight. Katie knows the property. Like any good real estate agent, she saw the house at the time Emily purchased it. She has not seen the redecorating. If you looked for a picture of the quintessential real estate agent in the dictionary, surely you would find one of Katie. She is vivacious and always on, done up to the nines, has information about every property in the area, is full of ideas, and exudes confidence. I have no doubt she will get the job done.

People have been trying to contact me about Emily's house since her funeral. Although I won't go so far as to say the vultures are circling, the people in the community are well aware that I am under a lot of pressure as winter is setting in and I live a substantial distance away. People seem to think they will get quite the bargain; that I will be forced to sell the place for a song. If the truth be known, I *am* under a lot of pressure. Following the big housing crisis that involved subprime mortgages of 2007 / 2008, real estate is not the ever-increasing price game it once was. I need to realize the appraised value of the house, just as I did for the van. Since Emily has left cash to beneficiaries, I am obligated to try my best to ensure they each get the monies left to them.

Our meeting with Katie goes well. She doesn't mind being forced to perch on a kitchen chair in the midst of boxes for recycle, boxes for the food bank, bags of clothes for charity, and bags of garbage. My puppy decides to hold court by sitting on Katie's knee throughout most of our meeting. She understands the work involved as we divest the property of anything personal. She knows we have to go through everything ourselves before selling the contents of the house. I know what Emily paid for the house, what is owed on the mortgage, and what I need to get in cash after the bills are paid. We decide on a price. Katie faxes the paperwork to me when I am back at home. She has clients who are looking for a house just like Emily's. They have been searching for a while now and Katie looks forward to bringing them. I am really concerned about the state of the house. Not only is it not staged for showing, but it is piled high with the personal effects of a dead person. I am afraid we might just blow our best chance to sell. Katie assures me they will look at the real estate and not the contents. We are both wrong. I do not have to worry as the potential buyers want to purchase some of the contents and Katie doesn't have to worry because exposing her client to the contents helps to cinch the sale.

You never know how someone else will see a piece of property. Many cannot see past a red wall or a lot of clutter. Others want the red wall and to buy the clutter. In the end, Emily's mausoleum dining room, the one that never saw a dinner party, sells the house, and all that furniture is included in the price. Possession is scheduled for the end of March, so this whole transaction does not take place overnight; and yes, they do try to low-ball me initially with an outrageous offer, but we eventually come to terms, with Katie's help. The sale of the house is a great relief after a long winter of managing it, but then the push is on to dispose of the contents and turn over the keys.

The cats dealt with, there are three other major areas of concern inside the house: the food stuffs, Emily's personal effects, and all the paperwork deposited in nooks and crannies absolutely everywhere. It all has to be sorted and cleared from the property before I can call in an appraiser to formally value the contents and assist me in preparation for auction. I am anxious to get the work done before Christmas so the clothes and food can go to charity.

Her computer and her MasterCard prove the most troubling when it comes to her paperwork. My husband's skills with the computer lead us to a myriad of online accounts for computer games, having memberships automatically charged to Emily's credit card. The cancellation of such charges is difficult, to say the least. It is only through hours of hard work and intense investigation on David's part, that we are able to successfully shut down all of her cyberspace accounts.

From the time Emily died until possession date on the sale of the property, my husband and I spend one hundred and seventy hours in the house packing, sorting, and cleaning. This does not include any work done by the caretaker in the yard, Henry and Violet's work, or any work I do from home. Make no mistake, if you accept the task of executor, expect it to be very hands on. You are responsible for securing the property and the effects, for ensuring that the most money is realized for the estate and the beneficiaries, and for the distribution of items. You will be accountable to Probate Court. I cannot accomplish my tasks without the total support of my husband, Emily's neighbours Violet and Henry, our talented real estate agent, and an appraiser / auctioneer of impeccable reputation. These are the only people who share that inner circle of executing Emily's will.

One of the most enlightening things I learn throughout this experience is that an estate is a living thing, like a business. Just because a person dies, it does not mean their estate does not have to carry out the ongoing responsibilities of the deceased. So in the end, as simplistic as it may appear, my role is to carry on in Emily's stead. I am to ensure her affairs are in order before bank accounts can be closed, before taxes are no longer due, and until bills stop turning up in the mail.

It sounds simple enough, but executorship is not an open book of public information. There are no written rules of engagement and no one I know has ever talked in detail about their experiences.

On the day of her death, going to Albertville to meet with the bank that holds both Emily's mortgage and her investment portfolio proves to be the polar opposite of my initial experience with her bank in Elmsville, where they refused to see me at all. I am quickly ushered into a private office and meet with the assistant branch manager, a middle aged, highly efficient and soft spoken woman, empathetic and anxious to help. She accepts a certified copy of the will along with my identification with grace. I may drop off the death certificate at my convenience.

This is where I learn the ins and outs of estate accounts and probate. Before I am able to have access to any of Emily's existing funds, the will has to be probated. This means the probate court must approve me to take over the management of the estate and allow the banks to release Emily's funds. It will give me permission to execute the will, collect money, pay bills, distribute assets, sell assets, and deal with any beneficiaries. What we are able to do during this encounter is establish an estate account so I can ensure any monies owed to Emily from pensions will be deposited there. Once probate occurs, the banks will release the funds in the existing accounts and they will be transferred to the new estate account over which I will have sole signing authority. The old accounts in Emily's name will be closed. Now, I feel I am finally getting somewhere.

Once we set up the new account and get a print out of her current account from which her mortgage payment is withdrawn, we take advantage of the one month a year holiday on the mortgage and eliminate the November payment. Then, the assistant manager introduces me to the funds manager who oversees Emily's investment portfolio. He has no idea Emily has passed away and as a result becomes my first notification of her death to someone who knows her well, although his staff has prepared him in advance of my entrance. This is when the shock and strain starts to get the best of me. I am exhausted and my emotions are lying raw on the surface of my skin. I am shocked and numb as I come to understand the magnitude of the situation in which I find myself. The least little touch, physical or figural, would be more than I can bear. Emily's funds manager has been her friend and thinks the world of her. He stands when I enter the office, leaning over the desk to offer his hand. His pain is visible in his eyes and it is all I can do not to simply sit in the cozy comfort of his hushed office and weep. We talk about Emily. He gets me the paperwork I need. We plan on a simple liquidation of the fund and will drop the proceeds (a mere fraction of the money she received when Rob died) into the estate account once approval from probate court is obtained. When I leave that second bank, I am worn out, but somehow comforted. I will work with contacts here who are trustworthy and who will listen.

My second visit, at the appointed time, to the bank in Elmsville, is as challenging as the first time. They have their rules and they follow them to the letter. Apparently, having an emotional connection is a frowned upon state of affairs in this organization. In the end, they get what they need and, ultimately, so do I. This is the end of my work with this bank.

I feel as though I accomplished a great deal on that first day. The lawyer has told me to secure Emily's property and I feel I have done that. So, I call the lawyer to report my progress and to let him know we can proceed with probate as soon as possible. I am very anxious, as Emily has big bills to pay. I have a lot of sorting to do, but I know she has money owing and do not want bill collection to hang over me. Not so fast – in order to apply for probate, a form must be filled out that will estimate with a certain level of detail, the overall value of the estate. He will send me a copy of the form via email or I can obtain a copy on line via the government website. I need to complete the form and send it to him so that he can proceed to court. The form will summarize all of Emily's assets. This would be difficult if I had to do it for myself, let alone for someone else! This is yet another unfamiliar task, and a daunting one at that, to add to my list.

The lawyer for the estate, a voice on the phone and an email correspondent, operates on a "need to know" basis throughout the whole process. He gives me information only when circumstances appear to be warranted from his perspective. This is more than a little frustrating for me as I am a planner. He seems to think executors will get overwhelmed with the details, but I want to know ahead of time what events will require coordinating and what kind of planning will be necessary. I am regularly blindsided with additional tasks, to me, propelled from out of nowhere. I oftentimes wish for some sort of cheat sheet – a list of things that will be required (demanded) of me. I often think to myself, "Why didn't you tell me that before?"; "When am I supposed to get time to do that?"; "I thought we were finished with that already." In all fairness, this lawyer does not know me and did not know Emily. He did not write the will. He has no idea if I am capable or not. His error is in not making an attempt to find out. It is much further down the road before he ever meets with me or assesses my abilities as an executrix.

The Probate Court form is used to provide an estimate of value of an inventory of the estate. This includes her house, her vehicle, the cash in her bank accounts, and all of her possessions. I do not have to have an exact accounting, but probate taxes will be owed and paid as a percentage of my totals. The lawyer tells me not to estimate too high as it will take a long time to recover any over payments of taxes, but not to estimate too low, or the estate will owe more taxes later down the line. I invest a considerable amount of time to ensure I get as close as possible to the value of her things, including what I expect in insurance monies and what I think we will realize upon liquidation. Just try looking around someone else's house sometime and see if you can pinpoint a value. What a job! Probate is granted to me on November 24, just eleven days after Emily's death. The lawyer suggests this is some kind of record, but I am not interested in lingering over any aspect of the process. I need control. I cannot move forward without power. Eleven days in and the probate taxes and legal fees, along with the costs of the funeral, have exceeded the money Emily has in her bank accounts for which I am still awaiting access. In addition, her investment is only enough to pay off the mortgage. I am very worried that I will have trouble realizing the cash needed to fulfil the substantial bequests Emily has left in her will.

The end of the year fast approaches and that means tax time. Every year, as I did my own tax return, I noticed the box: "If this return is for a deceased person, enter the date of death." I never really thought about the ramifications of that box until now. So, my first question is whether it is necessary to engage an accountant or if I can manage myself. I have always done my own taxes. I start to research. I find Emily's last return to use as a guide. The first one will be straightforward. Eventually, I will have to do what are called T3 Trust returns to reflect income to the estate, but I don't anticipate there will be much besides a CPP death benefit that will not come in until early in 2010, any insurance payouts, and any interest earned. I make up my mind then and there not to invest any of Emily's money or I will be doing T3 Trust returns indefinitely. In my reading, I determine I cannot close the estate without a Revenue Canada Clearance Certificate – the holy grail of estate taxation. This clears the estate (and the executor) of any further obligations to the tax department. My goal is to get that Clearance Certificate in as timely a manner as possible.

Revenue Canada helps me a lot with this. When I call and tell them I am managing an estate, I am put in touch with a group of employees whose sole purpose is to deal with the tax returns of the dead. They are much nicer on the phone than the regular tax folks. They must take a course in active listening or empathetic responses or something. They employ a sense of humour, strategically, of course, and I learn a great deal. They assure me I am perfectly capable of doing the estate taxes myself and they will be happy to help in any way they can. Throughout this whole process, Revenue Canada proves to be a little star to light a path that is often very dim and cluttered with obstacles of one sort or another. I must tell you that receiving that Clearance Certificate (little did I know it would take almost a year from the time Emily died) is as rewarding as almost anything I have ever done. There are challenges in the execution of Emily's will, some that prove insurmountable, but this is one particular area where I take control and complete all tasks to the best of my ability. I am not forced to pay huge professional costs and for this I am grateful. The legal fees, appraisal fees, court fees, real estate fees, and auction fees often appear poised to consume this relatively small estate.

Over the years, once I agreed to be Emily's executrix, she often teased me about a safety deposit box she and Rob maintained since they left their posting in Waterbury, Alberta back in the 1980s. She informed me the box was filled with valuable coins and dreamt of a road trip where she and I would cross the country and clean out that box. I even suggested, once, that we take the train to Edmonton and then the bus to Waterbury. She just laughed. Sure enough, as I root through Emily's paperwork during those first days following her death, I discover the lease for two boxes at the Credit Union in Waterbury. Emily and Rob had faithfully been paying the annual fees for almost thirty years.

I shudder to think what the financial implications to the estate will be if I have to fly to Waterbury, Alberta to open safety deposit boxes. So, I do the only thing I can do at the time. I called the bank and asked to speak to the manager. Thank God for flat fee long distance packages. Throughout this whole process, I just pick up the phone and make a call, and believe me, I am not shy, regardless of the circumstances. Kathy Lewinski is both available and kind. From her voice, I imagine her as cute and perky, a no nonsense kind of girl in short skirts and stilettos, wearing frilly blouses and looking a lot less like a bank manager than you might expect until you start to listen to what she has to say. She makes it clear I will have to appear with the keys, Emily's death certificate and a copy of the will. Other than that, there will be absolutely no problem. I have no keys. Now, I have all kinds of keys that must have intimate relationships with objects I may likely never discover, but certainly no safety deposit box keys. Well now, this is a horse of a different colour. If I have no keys, and the estate is not prepared to pay for the boxes in perpetuity, they will have to be opened by a locksmith under the auspices of a lawyer and two bank officials. The estate will have to foot the bill. Since I am in no great hurry to incur additional estate expenses right away, we decide I will send the required support documents via fax and she will talk to her superiors about the idea of opening up the boxes. A little miracle in the key department would save a lot of locksmith money.

Whenever my husband or I attempt to find something in her house, or solve some problem that percolates to the surface, we always say we are going to try and channel Emily. We both do the same thing. We work methodically and with extreme focus. What would Emily do? Where could Emily have been at the time? What could Emily have been thinking? One afternoon, about two weeks after my conversation with Ms. Lewinski, my husband vacuums the floors in our house while I am at my office. Under the work table in the back room is that file box Emily had initially been so conscientious about managing. It is empty now, as I have moved everything to a bigger storage container. Her paperwork has been re-sorted to better comply with my sense of organization. Why have I not thrown that file box out? I have no intention of using it again. It's falling apart. David lifts it to clean the floor, and feels compelled, by some unknown force, to give the thing a quick shake. Where would Emily keep those safety deposit keys so we could find them easily? They rattle from a fold in a divider at the bottom of the box. It is like discovering the crown jewels! We can now proceed to convince the Credit Union that if we send them the keys, they can open the boxes and forward the contents. Still lots of hurtles to jump, but this is likely the biggest one of all put behind us.

I call Ms. Lewinski that night and we put together a plan. I will courier the keys to her. The boxes will be opened, but only in the presence of another bank official besides herself as well as a legal representative for the estate. The bank cannot be held accountable for the contents. They will photograph and list everything and send it off to me. We can make arrangements for shipping after that. She recommends a law firm that happens to be located directly across the street from the bank. I talk to the estate lawyer. I ask that he write the Waterbury lawyer to formally engage his services. Oh, and by the way, we will need a detailed list of the contents so that the formal asset appraisal can include those items. The contents are coins and all the coins are left to one person, but it seems that does not matter. For final probate, a complete list with detailed values will have to be completed by a licensed appraiser and forwarded to the probate court. Probate taxes have only been paid on my estimate and the final probate tax figure depends on a detailed appraisal. Just when I think I am making some progress, my "to do" list gets hit with yet another addendum. I silently wonder when I would have discovered this tidbit of information if I had not called him with the safety deposit box issue.

So, in the end, the Waterbury Credit Union (read Ms. Lewinski) helps me more than I can even describe. She manages everything on her end. She schedules the lawyer, supervises completion of the inventory, and engages her staff to help pack and ship the boxes. She communicates clearly and often with me. She is a rock, as well as a delightful contact. The lawyer from across the street goes over and they open the boxes. They take pictures and count all the coins and there are a lot. Emily and Rob had roll upon roll of nickels and dimes filling one huge box. It appears they assumed these coins, issued for an occasion or celebration, would eventually increase in value. Just like the dolls from Zellers, there is little chance of that happening in our lifetime. The total value is only $1,723.37 but they have to be shipped in five different parcels weighing slightly less than ten kilograms each, which is the maximum shipping weight for coinage. The shipping, insurance, and costs to pack up result in charges from the Waterbury Credit Union of just under $300.00. The lawyer charges me $825.00 to walk across the street, observe opening the boxes and send the list compiled by the bank employees to my lawyer. When Ms. Lewinski discovers the size of the legal bill, she quickly determines that she and her staff can reopen and pack up the safety deposit box contents without further services from this lawyer. I send her flowers. So there you have it - $1,723.37 worth of coins costs the estate $1,125.00 to retrieve and get to Nova Scotia.

And then there is the second box. Its opening leads to yet another surprise.

At this point I want to take a moment and point out what is probably quite obvious. As an executor, you will likely be living your life in circumstances quite similar to me. I work full time, so from early morning until late afternoon, my existence belongs (in my case) to the provincial government. I also travel in my job, meaning I log a fair chunk of overtime as well. I have family like everyone else and there are those standard Christmas and birthday obligations. Life happens. During this period, in early February, one of my favourite aunts passes away. I have been travelling to see her as often as possible, including one stormy weekend where we go across the province to Elmsville and work at Emily's all day and then head to the city to see my aunt before driving home. The roads are a glare of ice and there are cars in the ditch everywhere, but I have to make the best use of the free days I have. When I get the call that she has died, I am at the other end of the province, training staff, and I rush home after work to be able to attend her funeral the next day. At the time, my workload is doubled, as I am covering a vacant position. According to my calendars, I log approximately sixty hours per month relating to Emily's estate for the first three months and then thirty-five hours a month for the next three. Although things slow down after the house is sold and the assets liquidated, just when I think we are ready to finalize the estate, the lawyer calls with yet another task. I suppose I can farm out more work to others, but that will cost more money than the estate is able to support.

Friends of mine adopted a baby relatively late in life. They had previously been childless. When their little girl was three years old, my friend said to me that she had never been more tired. She had no idea how much work she had gotten herself into and she did not think anyone could have ever explained it to her ahead of time. This might well be a parallel circumstance.

Chapter 7
Behind Closed Doors

Violet deals with Emily's clothes. She trudges through the snow between their adjoining back yards to the house every day and toils away for a few hours. She methodically cleans out drawers and closets, packing items into green garbage bags for pickup by a local charity. Lingerie goes into the garbage. Anything else requiring repairs is trashed as well. Emily has clothes in every size imaginable. She has more than fifty pairs of shoes and a couple of dozen coats. Some garments have never had the tags removed. She has purses that still have their paper packing inside. Every closet in her three thousand square foot Cape Cod home is stuffed with clothes. In the end, there are ninety-three green garbage bags that wait stoically for the charity pickup van. I stand at the top of the utility room stairs and gaze out over the garage floor, down on a sea of green sacks with their integral red ties, all neatly arranged in rows by Henry. They manage to look festive with that particular Christmas colour combination. They cover all the space where two cars could have parked. Violet and I are both completely baffled. In all the time we have known Emily, in all the conversations we have shared, she never once discussed shopping for clothes with either of us. It is a little unsettling to think she bought clothes at least weekly for years – way beyond the volume of most women without some sort of shopping addiction – and she never even mentioned a purchase. There are clothes from Sears, mall stores, The Shopping Channel, and mail order houses completely foreign to me. Whenever we met in Fiddlehead Bay for lunch (and this would only be a couple of times a year) she invariably had on something new and I would invariably remark on her outfit. She would reply that she had picked something up the last time she had been shopping. To look at that sea of green on the garage floor, I start to understand just how much shopping Emily had actually been doing. Violet does an unbelievable job. For days, she worked – folded, sorted, packed – felt Emily's presence in the house and in the clothes, smelled her scent, touched her life in garment after garment. It is a sacrifice of time and an exercise in fortitude. I am forever grateful she volunteered for a task that I am not sure I could have done myself.

I clean out Emily's dresser. All she ever wore for jewellery were her wedding rings and a basic pair of gold hoop earrings in her pierced ears. I never saw her in anything else, even the odd time when she dressed up for an occasion. Her dresser drawers are filled with boxes of rings, necklaces, earrings, and evening bags wrapped in tissue - trimmings of another life and another place - trappings of a happier time.

Next, we tackle the food and contents of the cupboards. David and I spend the three weekends leading up to Christmas dealing with food and household supplies. The Elmsville Food Bank tells us they will take absolutely anything that is unopened, even frozen things, cleaning products and toiletries. Everything else has to be disposed of properly through recycling. Our confirmation of Emily's hoarding tendencies happen as we plod our way through this task.

Let's start with the sinks. I have two bathrooms and a kitchen sink in my house. I keep a set of cleaning products under the kitchen sink and on the designated day, the supplies come out and all the washing areas of the house get cleaned. Emily's methodology is slightly different. She has three bathrooms as well as kitchen and laundry room sinks. Under each sink is a complete set of cleaning supplies – a foam cleanser, a clear cleanser, a variation of a green product, Ajax, and Mr. Clean. Under each sink is an unopened product to match the one that is opened. Emily, when she cleaned house, obviously did not want to lug her little bucket of cleaning supplies from one bathroom or sink to another. So, just to be clear, there are ten bottles or cans of cleaning supplies under each of five sinks. Anything unopened can go to the Food Bank. The open products have to be disposed of, the containers washed, and everything properly sorted.

Toiletries are much the same. Whatever Emily liked, she had one open and a couple more as backup. There are also more than a dozen different shampoos and conditioners stuffed into cupboard drawers in bathrooms. They were obviously tried and not liked. Do you know it takes about twenty minutes, and I cannot begin to tell you how much water, to clean out a half empty bottle of shampoo? I have trouble believing I am being a friend to my environment.

Emily's upright freezer is a sight to behold. It is thirty-four inches wide and holds twenty-four cubic feet of contents. It was the biggest available model at the time. It is so full that when I open the door, things tumble out. A shelf has collapsed under the weight of frozen packages and things are spread every which way. She has five crown roasts. She has twenty-two boxes of frozen candy – different kinds of things like Toffifay and Ganongs. Each is opened and has a few pieces taken. I ponder the conflicts that must have gone on in Emily's mind. She would buy things on the chance she would have company, although I was never offered anything like this when I was there. She probably wondered if she offered candy to people, if they would think she, a diabetic, should not have such stuff in the house. Why would someone, anyone besides perhaps Rachel Ray or Martha Stewart, need to have five crown roasts on hand? No matter how good the sale, isn't buying five defeating the purpose? Emily did not drink coffee, although she would make it for other people when they came to visit. She has more than ten pounds of coffee in the freezer including a number of different flavoured types. The shelves are crammed with every type of vegetable that you can possibly imagine that is able to be purchased frozen in a bag, with duplicates where one bag is opened and the other is not. It takes ten hours of work for

David and I to empty the freezer of everything, dispose of the opened things, and repack it with the unopened products. We save those for the food bank and clean the freezer after they come for the pick up.

Next we hit the kitchen cupboards. I start with the pantry. This is one of those floor to ceiling affairs that has shelves on the doors and turn around shelving on the inside. Just when I think I have seen it all, a shelf spins around and there's more. This cabinet holds tea, cooking supplies like oil, grains, rice, as well as her sushi supplies, cake decorating supplies, and any exotic ingredients not requiring refrigeration. I am not trying to be evasive here but there are many things in that cupboard I cannot identify even after reading the label. She has ten different kinds of cooking oil. Each example has one open bottle as well as an unopened one. There are more than sixty kinds of tea. Now, Emily was a tea lover. We always visited the tea shop when we were in Fiddlehead Bay and she always managed to find a few new ones to try, but sixty? I cannot believe my eyes. Most boxes or bags are opened and a sample or two removed.

What I learn about my friend is this: Emily would find a recipe with lots of unusual ingredients and shop for each item. She would come home, try the recipe, and in most cases, never revisit that product again. If she liked something, she bought lots of it so she would never, ever, run out. If she didn't like it, she would never throw it out, unless it was perishable, and judging by the refrigerator there was no guarantee of that. She purchased food as if she would do mountains of baking for a fundraiser or have half the town for dinner, but she did neither. There was not a square inch of space anywhere in her kitchen for more food. Just to give you an example, I have a bread maker which I love and I make my own bread and have for years, mostly due to food allergies. I would take Emily the occasional loaf when going over for a visit. Emily got a bread maker just like mine one fall, a couple of years before she died. She bought many, many cook books and baked bread for all of her rug hooking buddies and her Order of Women's Collective friends. She baked some fancy bread, using all kinds of exotic flours, grains, and added ingredients like currents and dried apricots. She was quite proud of herself, telling me all about delivering her creations the week before the holidays. She never used the bread maker again after that Christmas. I find most of the ingredients in the pantry, the machine in the laundry room closet, and the cook books at the back of her book shelf. Like all of her crafts with the exception of rug hooking, Emily bought all the paraphernalia, did the job, did it well, and then did not do it again.

We call the president of the local food bank the week before Christmas. He says he will come over with his car. As I look at the cardboard boxes carpeting the kitchen floor, the laundry room floor, and most of the family room, I tell him I think a car will not do the trick. He offers to bring his wife's van. I tell him I think a truck might be a better option and perhaps he needs to bring along a friend. He arrives a couple of hours later with a three-quarter ton pickup and a large gentleman to help. We load the vehicle completely, two boxes deep. He says it will be the best Christmas the food bank has ever seen, but he wishes they had Emily back instead.

On New Year's Eve, David and I are back at Emily's, sorting again. Papers come next. Until this time, I always thought a disorganized filing system is better than no filing system at all. Emily has three substantial filing cabinets and two desks. She also has storage drawers in her converted computer room / office. There is absolutely no rhyme or reason to what I find in any paperwork storage facility. I start by searching out what I need like the latest information from every bank account and investment, the most recent bill from every charge card and account, any and all correspondence related to pensions, insurance, health care, and the military. I bring home boxes of loose papers I find stuffed in file cabinets, stacked on desks, and rammed in drawers. I sit at home and go through each piece of paper to determine what is needed and what can be safely shredded. She stopped keeping up with that critical file folder of relevant papers. I am left with three years of bills, bank statements, and correspondence through which to sift. I finally give up harbouring any thoughts of completion. Every time I feel I have a handle on the paperwork, we go back to the house, I open a drawer, and just like the pantry, there lies another something. While others, no doubt, primp for a party or curl up by their fire ready to usher in 2010, David and I stop at the local grocery store and pick up a couple of frozen dinners. We get a bottle of wine and make our way back to Emily's through the icy, quiet streets of the little town. We sit in her family room and listen to CBC on the radio and eat something from a box with not enough vegetables and way too much salt, as we plan our next attacks before the weekend is over and we are again forced to navigate the winter roads back across the province.

Two other areas of the house cry out for attention. The first is the office upstairs. Emily had what was the third bedroom renovated with two walls of shelves and base cabinets, leaving room for her exerciser and her computer desk. All the shelves are filled with Chalet glass. Shortly before Rob died, Emily decided she would start a new collection and chose what I consider to be the most hideous glass known to man. It is that heavy, blown junk that has flutes and sprays. It is unsuitable for anything except sitting on a shelf or in the middle of a coffee table and never intended for use. Each piece seems to weigh a ton. She has more than one hundred pieces. When I eventually take the auctioneer on a tour of the house, I fear he is going to quit on principle when he comes across that glass. Two pieces together won't even pack fully in one box as they are all so oddly shaped. Well, every drawer and cupboard underneath the shelves is filled with office materials. Emily has enough paper, envelopes, ledgers, clips, elastics, sticky notes, and file folders to keep Staples in business. It was her intention, in the beginning, to sell her collections piece by piece on Ebay, so I assume she decided to outfit her office for this major operation. There are knocked down boxes in every size, a postage machine, a scanner and a copier. She never posted one item for sale on the Internet, ever. She has a beautiful digital camera and a photography tent to take pictures of items so there would be no background visible. They were never used. The tent is still in its original box. Poor Emily. Much like Rob, when it came to actually doing a task that would generate money, she was all about the planning but not about the execution. She started out well, as in when she decided to try a new craft, but once the office was ready to go, she faded in the back stretch just when the real work was ready to commence.

The condition of her computer is troubling to say the least. Emily obviously had stomach problems she never shared with me. There are Tums everywhere. It seems she ate them like candy. I find them in every room of the house, both loose and in packages big and small. I know she wasn't using them as candy, because there are empty boxes of candy hidden all over the office as well. It appears Emily was playing Internet games into the wee hours of the morning and eating candy. Her stomach would bother her, so she would switch to the Tums. Then she would wonder why her sugars were so high when she tested at breakfast time. She definitely had her secrets.

The last area of the house that requires mentioning is the basement. It is a horror on a number of levels. When Emily moved into her dream house from The Inn, she had all her collectible dolls, Santas, and related paraphernalia stacked into what had once been a recreation room in the basement. All of Rob's tools and all of their hobby supplies and equipment are in the open part of the basement. There is another small room and all the belongings of her parents are piled in that room. There are boxes, bags, and wardrobes reaching to the ceiling in all three areas. In addition, the cats had their litter box down there. In the last months of her life, Emily was obviously not well because the cats (her most beloved possessions) were not cared for in the pristine manner to which they had no doubt become accustomed. The cats threw up a lot, it seems, and Emily simply chose to ignore that issue. So, the Molly Maids refuse to clean the basement floor, which amounts to scrubbing around the piles of possessions and cleaning up evidence of cat issues. With our focus on the upstairs, David and I leave the basement until it is time to let other people in the house besides Violet and Henry. David scrubs the floors with bleach before Katie brings any potential buyers through, and I start taking stock of what exactly confronts us down in the caves of possessions and collectibles below.

I suppose, by this point, you are suitably aghast at the life-style of my dear friend, Emily. I really do not want you to be. This is not my intention as I provide some of the most disturbing details you have read thus far. My intent is not to cast aspersions on the memory of Emily, but as much as it pains me to reveal the condition of her home and her finances, this sordid and sad element of the story must be revealed so that you may appreciate the gravity of my circumstance. I cannot just hire somebody to come into her house and sort through her possessions. All of her assets have to be protected for the value of the estate to be realized. Yes, I get Molly Maids to clean the floors, furniture, and countertops in the main part of the house so we are not scuffing through cat hair everywhere we go and I am able to stay overnight without having an asthma attack, but that is the limit of outside intervention. Even with Molly Maids, David stayed on site and supervised during the process for security purposes. I have to look at each piece of paper, handle everything of potential value, and dispose properly of anything that cannot be sold. I have a responsibility to all the beneficiaries to liquidate Emily's assets in the most effective way possible. I learn a lot about my friend throughout this exercise. I see clearly her loneliness and longing wrapped in the accumulation of food and the trappings of a life with Rob that no longer existed, ending in a neglect for all but the very basics and finally, in the neglect of even those.

Chapter 8

Searches

Emily leaves a substantial bequest to a gentleman whose name is Gregory Creighton. I have chosen not to document exact figures regarding the estate, but it suffices to say his bequest would be a windfall for an ordinary working person of middle class means. I do not know who this person is. None of the other beneficiaries know him and so my search starts, virtually from the time of initial notification. In Emily's address book, I find someone whose name is Albert Creighton and I call him. I identify myself as the executrix for the estate of Emily Maxwell and say I am calling to inform him of Emily's sudden death. Of course, he is shocked and upset. He was in the military with the Maxwells and has maintained contact with them over all these years, exchanging Christmas cards and the like. So, does he know Gregory and where I can find him?

Gregory is Albert's son by birth. He and his first wife split up and struggled through a rather messy divorce when Gregory was four. Rob and Emily, as godparents, took the child in with the hopes of adopting him. It all fell through when Gregory's mother returned to retrieve him about eight months later. Mother and son disappeared for some time. She eventually gave Gregory up for adoption to an unknown family when he was seven or eight years old but that is all his birth father knows. Albert says he will be happy to try and get information from Manitoba Child Find but there's one small glitch. He cannot remember Gregory's date of birth and without this information, there is nothing he is able to do to help. He has no clue as to the current location of his first wife, either. Frankly, he does not know if she is alive or dead.

Little of this story is ringing any bells with me. When Emily originally showed me her will, I asked who this Gregory person was and she said he was their godson. The other beneficiaries are recognizable to me as some attended Rob's funeral and their names are familiar. Given the chance for a "do over" as executrix, I would quiz Emily a bit more about this person and probably discover she had no idea on earth as to his location. At the time, reading over her will while she stands beside me is akin to peeking in her dresser drawers while she watches from the doorway. It just seems so personal. The single biggest mistake I make when I take on this job for Emily is not asking her more questions. I simply have to find this man.

As noted, I personally handle every piece of paper in the house. As executrix, it is imperative I ensure nothing is lost or forgotten as I assemble Emily's estate for liquidation. The contents are pulled out of every box and every folder. A decision is made about each and every scrap. After countless hours where I open, sort, shred, decide, and refile, we come upon an Apple computer box that originally held installation gear for Emily's Mac. I start to go through the box only to discover old Polaroid snapshots tossed in the bottom and, other than these, it is empty. I stand at the kitchen counter looking at snaps of a little boy; stacks of fading photos. I catch myself forgetting to breathe as I stand under the glare of the kitchen island light and look at this slice of the Maxwells' life. I find a birth announcement. It is one of those old fashioned cards that parents used to send to their friends long before they could post birth pictures on Facebook. It's stuck between the bottom flaps of the box. Gregory Matthew Jonathan Creighton was born in Lakeland, Manitoba on December 10, 1976 and weighted eight pounds, zero ounces. If I tell you I am flabbergasted, it will be more than a significant understatement. My hands shake. My eyes well with tears. I start yelling for my husband. I never do figure out why this birth announcement and the snapshots are in a relatively new box in the basement. Had Emily started to organize these old things she had held on to for so many years? I cannot fathom. The pictures are of Gregory with Emily and Rob during the time he lived with them; of a camping trip in their big, old RV; of them at the Ottawa Exhibition; of him asleep, playing ball, and in his Halloween costume. He is four years old in the photos. Later on, in a box of cards (Emily and Rob saved every card they had ever given one another over the years and there are hundreds of them), I find a letter from Gregory's birth father and step mother. They thank Emily and Rob over and over for saving this little boy from an unpredictable and unreliable future. With evidence in hand, I feel confident I will be able to find this young man who is now almost thirty-four years old.

I again talk to Albert Creighton who readily agrees to contact Manitoba Child Find and request information on his child who has been adopted. He will fill out all the forms and once he gets any information, he will forward it to me. In the meantime, I start Internet searching. This sounds easy, but really is not. Gregory could be anywhere. He could now have the same name as his adoptive parents. He could have moved to the United States or even to Europe. If a military family is involved, he could be just about anywhere. Eventually, as in months later, I receive information from Manitoba via Albert Creighton. Gregory was adopted into a Koehler family in 1986 and his name was legally changed to Koehler by the adoption court in Creit River, Manitoba. Any identifying information about the Koehlers, who adopted Gregory, is blacked out on the document. The forms are redacted to protect the privacy of the adoptive parents, I assume. I feel excited, invigorated, and frustrated all at the same time. When I call the birth father to thank him, he tells me he actually located Gregory's birth mother and all she is able to add to our information is that she is pretty sure when she dropped Gregory off at the social services office in Lakeland, it was a man in a uniform waiting to pick him up. Big help.

The most haunting thing happens to me as I sift through the piles and piles of basement storage items. Tucked away among Emily's mother's things is a cassette tape, labelled in Emily's distinctive handwriting. It says "Adoption of Gregory Discussion". I take it home, find my old cassette player I used when I interviewed care givers for my Masters thesis, and I curl up with a cup of tea to listen. Emily and Rob are talking about life changing consequences if they adopt a troubled four year old boy, their godson. I imagine them at the kitchen table. I can hear the spoon clink on the cup as tea is stirred. I can hear the click of the lighter and the smoky sigh of that first puff. Their voices float across my living room as if I could look up and see them at the table across from me. It is eerie at best. I feel strangely uncomfortable, again, guilty for peeking behind a very private curtain. They talk to one another about what might happen if they do this, and about the support they might or might not receive from their own families as well as the child's maternal grandmother. They talk about their fear of loving Gregory so much and then his unpredictable mother returning to scoop him up, never to be seen again. They talk about the challenges with his behaviour. It sounds as though he is a troubled child indeed. They make their decision to accept him into their home and to apply for permanent adoption, on that tape, as I listen. It could easily be argued this was the single biggest decision of their married life. Why do I not know about any of this? Obviously, Emily buried her feelings of loss and pain in a deep, dark and protected part of her heart. Buried like the tape, itself. I never find anyone who is able to provide additional details.

Over the next six months, in my spare time and whenever I think about it, I search for Gregory or information about Gregory. I call all Koehler listings in both Creit River and Lakeland, Manitoba. No one to whom I talk can even tell me that the story of someone in their family adopting an eight year old sounds familiar. Families would know if someone, even a distant relative, adopted a child of this age. It is just not that common. I call every G. Koehler in Manitoba to no avail. I tend to put a lot of stock in family history and am lucky enough to have the opportunity to talk to a long time resident of Creit River. She is a member of the Koehler family and knows everybody. Although elderly and with a care giver, she is alert, oriented, and well able to speak with me on the telephone. She talks about her family and tells me categorically that if anyone named Koehler adopted a ten year old and has been a member of her community, she would remember. I believe her.

In my search, I use Google Scholar, PIPL, Lexus Nexus news, Blog search engine, Kijiji, and Academic Information search engines. I find nothing using all kinds of variations of Gregory's name both before and after adoption. On Facebook, I research all G. Koehler listings and review friends' lists of all Koehler listings I can find from Manitoba. I search Canadian and American obituary sites, to which I can obtain access. Upon recommendation from the RCMP Missing Persons Unit, I write the Federal Government National Search Unit. They are able to access Federal data bases like CPP and Revenue Canada. If they find the person, they will send them a letter to request the missing person contact the person searching for them. I receive a confirmation that my information had been received by them but they provide no follow-up as to the success of their search for confidentiality reasons. I have heard nothing in over two years. I search the Internet for missing persons and find nothing. I search information on both Creit River and Lakeland High School alumni and find nothing. I find a Koehler genealogy site and post a request for information there and get no response. I search ancestors.ca and come up empty. I advertise in the Creit River daily newspaper for a week and all northern Manitoba weekly newspapers. I never get a response. Finally, at considerable cost to the estate, I request from the governments of Manitoba, Ontario, and Alberta, that their death records be searched. None of them are able to find a death record under either surname.

So why do I do all this? Somebody has to, and like all other estate responsibilities, it inevitably falls to me. I guess I could hire a private detective. As executrix, it would be my prerogative but this would add a huge financial burden to the estate. The lawyer has no special ideas, no inside track. In the end, I talk to more than eight hundred people in five provinces. I log more than twenty-five hours just in making cold calls to absolute strangers. I hold my breath with every call. Would this be the one? I talk to some great guys who wish they might be *the* Gregory. I even talk to a Gregory Koehler born on December 10, but not adopted and no bells ring for him either. It is a daunting, and in the end, fruitless task. I am no further ahead than I was when I first found that birth announcement stuck to the fold in the bottom of a discarded Apple computer box.

What happens at this stage is a surprise at the time. Out of the blue, the lawyer tells me the Probate Court will have to be petitioned regarding what to do with Gregory's inheritance. It will not be divided up among the existing beneficiaries. It will not be included in the residual of the estate once everyone else is given their bequest. There is no provision in the will to direct the money back to the estate if this person cannot be found. Therefore, we have to ask the Probate Court for direction. For this I will be requested to provide a detailed report on all the efforts I made to contact this particular beneficiary. If the court determines I have done all I can do, then direction will be provided to the lawyer as to the steps required to handle the money Emily has left to Gregory. This is yet another task for which I have not been prepared in advance by the estate lawyer. I handle the job as best I can and provide the court with all the details of what was done, all the searches, the conversations with RCMP and others, the letters I wrote, and the records of advertising. Luckily, I can provide this because it is in my nature to keep records of some kind so that in some warped sense of reasoning, I feel more in control.

I am very troubled about the issue of Gregory, my inability to find him, and the lack of support from the very law office that created the will in the first place. Granted, the lawyer who composed the will is no longer there. I am not able to go to him to find out why Emily was not asked to try and locate this person before she decided to leave him a great deal of money. The lawyer assigned to the case needs to research the protocols and what is expected by Probate Court. Emily's estate has to pay for this research. The estate has to pay for filing the documents with the court and for the lawyer to attend court to determine the outcome. All this happens because no one asked Emily for contact information on her beneficiaries, or no one advised that she not leave monies to someone whose location she did not have. I think, since it is this very law office that is responsible for the compilation of the will, they need to bear some of the expense for the consequent problems in execution of that will. No such luck. Between the lawyer and me, it becomes a testy subject both in our email exchanges and telephone conversations.

In the end, all the money left to Gregory goes to the Nova Scotia Public Trustee. In essence, they keep the money on the chance that Gregory might miraculously turn up to claim his inheritance. What about the blasted truck collection he was left, as well? It appears the Public Trustee does not want the trucks. Big surprise. I make an offer to the lawyer. How about I find a buyer for the trucks? We can take the money realized from the sale and add it to the lump sum bequest. Will Probate Court and the Public Trustee accept this? It takes a month, but I finally get a signed statement from the solicitor of the Public Trustee whereby I have permission to sell the truck collection for a stipulated amount and to include that amount in the bequest to be turned over to them.

The bequest information is available publicly and apparently there are people who make their living trolling these websites and then looking for people who are missing and owed money. For a percentage, they reveal the source of their information. All this sounds a little sordid to me, smacking of back alleys and dimly lit bars with people who pass notes and use code words. I probably watch too much television. Maybe, someday, Gregory will turn up. Perhaps he will search for his birth father and that will lead him to me. Perhaps the National Search Unit has sent him my contact information and someday soon I will answer the phone and hear his voice. I have imagined it a thousand times. Whenever my telephone rings, a little part of my brain reminds me that it could be, it might be, what if it is – him. Until then, he remains a very big piece of unfinished business in my life.

Chapter 9
The Gun

In my somewhat biased opinion, guns are a curse. For me, the world would be a better place without any guns at all. The more control and regulation employed the better. I find bullets, and lots of them, in Emily's bedside tables. There are enough to fill a small grocery bag. We have the bullets. Now, where in God's name, is the gun (or guns)?

We comb through the house box by box, drawer by drawer, and closet by closet. We find nothing resembling a gun of any kind. Since the discovery of the bullets, I am reluctant to continue the inventory and clean-up, afraid that when I open a cupboard I might find the gun. Did Emily actually keep a loaded gun in the house? Did she feel she needed protection for some reason unknown to me? She never once mentioned ownership or the use of a gun, but she knew my feelings and probably thought better of advertising the fact. I know her military history, but she worked as a clerk and the thought never crossed my mind she would keep a loaded gun in the house for her protection. Now all bets are off, and I am extremely nervous.

I credit Dr. David Suzuki with saving my life. My husband and I were living in Peace River, Alberta in the 1980s. We owned a kitchen cabinet shop in the small northern community nestled in the valley of the junction of the Peace and Smokey Rivers. About nine o'clock one evening in late

September, I decided I wanted a copy of the local weekly newspaper. Accomplishing this task involved driving out of the valley to the top of the hill, about a seven kilometre trek. My husband didn't want to come with me, absorbed in a special episode of The Nature of Things with David Suzuki, so I went alone. On my way home, as I navigated back down the secondary road in the pitch black of the starless fall night, I heard the crack of a rifle shot. As I turned my head toward the passenger side of my SUV, a small hole appeared in the window just a split second before the window exploded, shattering into a million pieces. The cold air rushed into my vehicle and my left leg, just below my knee, felt suddenly as if someone was holding a flaming cigarette lighter against my skin. I pulled my car over to the side of the road and peered out the windowless passenger side at the ebony wash that enveloped me. My heart pounded and my hands shook. I knew, somehow instinctively, that I had been shot.

I practised as a mental health social worker in the area for many years and so was well known in town. My husband and I were currently business owners in the community and had a relatively high profile. Was someone trying to hurt me? Why? I did not want to panic. As I searched the darkness with unaccustomed eyes, the vision of someone approaching the car with a rifle popped into my head. It was definitely not safe to stay where I was. In a time without cell phones, I exercised my only option and I headed for home, a five kilometre drive. I was so afraid of passing out that I drove slowly and kept talking (read yelling) to myself all the way down the riverside road connecting our little subdivision to the highway. My leg burned with intensity far above anything I have ever felt before. I had no idea how badly I was hurt, how much blood I had already lost, or whether I would make it to the house. I did not go into town and to the hospital. We lived on the opposite side of the river and a large bridge spanned the mighty Peace. I would not take the chance of losing consciousness on the bridge as there was nowhere to go. At least, in heading for home, if worst came to worst, I could steer into the ditch and not into the wall of the bridge.

I drove into the yard and leaned on the horn until David appeared at the front door. He wondered at first why I didn't simply come inside if I had forgotten my purse. I screamed for him to come and help me. The left side of my body seemed paralysed, frozen. I couldn't lift my injured leg out of the vehicle without help. I couldn't press down or bear any weight on my leg. It felt strangely as if nothing was there. David ran. When he opened the door, the cab light illuminated the floor under the pedals; the mat puddled with blood. When he helped me out of my SUV and into his truck, blood pumped from the hole in my leg and flew across the driveway. David later told me he was afraid I would bleed to death before he got me to the hospital. I, on the other hand, at no time felt that the life was draining out of me. I was afraid, but not of dying. Shock is a wonderful thing for some people and an Achilles' heel for others. Some of us become quite lucid when in shock; able to think clearly and move forward. Others experience a kind of frozen inertia and coherent thought has to be done by someone else. Thankfully, I fall into the former category and found this out the hard way during a head-on car crash some twelve years earlier. I was completely in control on this night like no other in my life.

It took us about ten minutes to arrive at the hospital. I was bleeding quite badly and it did not take long for the local surgeon and our family physician (both at the hospital that night purely by coincidence) to assess the situation. The RCMP and the surgical and X-ray staff were called in at ten o'clock that Friday night. While I had surgery to remove a twenty-two long bullet embedded in the bone just under my left knee, my poor husband was grilled by the police and taken back up to the spot where I was shot, along with my bloody sweat pants containing the bullet hole, so the RCMP could determine the trajectory of the bullet. By early morning, they had retrieved the shell casings and knew where the shooter had been standing. By midday, they knew that two teenage boys had been shooting at wildlife and local dogs on and off all the previous day. They had killed a couple of squirrels and apparently some of the local residents had filed complaints with the Peace River police.

It was all over the news. Our radio station morning guy was a neighbour and he tried many times to get to see me that first day but the hospital was quite insistent. I was in critical condition and only my husband would be allowed in. By the end of the day, one of the two boys who had been on the hill - the one who had *not* shot me — went with his parents and turned himself in to the RCMP. They had bought the guns at a yard sale. For target practice, he and his friend had stood on the top of the hill and shot down at the lights on trucks that night. They missed. The bullet went through the passenger window of my SUV, grazed the dash and ended up lodged in the bone just below my left knee. If David had kept me company instead of watching The Nature of Things, he would have driven the car and that bullet would have entered my temple, just in front of my right ear. How the bullet did not ricochet off the dash and redirect into my chest will never be known either. Probably the speed of my moving forward changed the physics in some way I will likely never understand. The RCMP forensics team was amazed.

Recovery was slow and painful. Don't believe anything you see on television. I was in hospital for nine days receiving IV antibiotics every six hours. Then, I was on crutches. My leg was not broken but there was a bullet hole straight through the bone, like the eye of a needle. Slices of bone on either side of the bullet hole supported me. When I got home, I continued taking oral medication and had to change the dressing myself every day. I was deathly afraid of infection. The doctors made it clear that if I got a bone infection, I could lose my leg.

In the end, I am here to tell the tale and walking on both legs, but I have a profound abhorrence of guns of any kind. The search for a gun, hidden somewhere in Emily's house, is disturbing for me indeed.

Drawers or cupboards are the worst. I catch myself hovering in front of a hidden space, willing my hand to open it and rummage through the contents. It never gets easier until the day I receive word from Kathy Lewinski at the Waterbury

Credit Union that a gun has been found in one of the two safety deposit boxes. The bullets we have discovered are the proper size for the gun, so I am reasonably sure we are again safe in the house.

The estate lawyer often manages to find a way to complicate situations as we work through challenges that invariably arise within the process. I want the gun destroyed. I am not sure how that might happen, but I want it done. The lawyer thinks it might be valuable, so it needs to be appraised, a temporary transportation permit and registration obtained, and then it could be shipped across the country, probably by special couriers that carry guns. Is he kidding? Exactly who is making those arrangements and who is responsible for the gun once it gets here? I don't care what it's worth. I do not want to spend one nickel of estate money to get a gun to Nova Scotia from Alberta. Is my response irrational because I feel so strongly about guns? Don't care. Isn't going to happen. From this point, I take matters into my own hands regarding the gun.

The first thing I do is contact Jasper, my appraiser. With a picture of the gun, he provides a written value that will be used for probate purposes. After he reviews the pictures and takes into consideration the fact that the gun is relatively common and has not been cleaned or serviced in more than thirty years, he states it does not have any appreciable value. Hurrah!! There would be no financial consequences to the estate if it is destroyed. Now I can try and dispose of it without bringing it to Nova Scotia.

I expect the RCMP get many unusual calls in the run of a day. You have the standard moose on the highway, drunk on the street corner, overturned truck with chickens all over the road kind of call. Therefore, when I telephone the Waterbury detachment of the RCMP and speak with Constable MacLean, I think they have probably heard it all and my request will come as no surprise. Not so, it seems. I tell him my sad little tale of woe - that I am the executrix of this estate; that Emily and Rob lived in Waterbury many years before; that there is a gun in a safety deposit box at the Credit Union in town and I would like a representative from the force to go to the bank, get the gun, and destroy it on my behalf. No big deal. He has some questions. Did I have a firearms licence? Now, why would I have one of those? I hate guns and this gun is not mine. Was the gun licensed to Rob or Emily? I hardly think so since they had not laid eyes on it for thirty years. Perhaps a copy of the most recent, although seriously outdated, licence will be with the gun. Would I arrive in Waterbury to accompany him to the bank? No, but Kathy Lewinski will act on my behalf with the permission of her superiors. At this point, hope fades that I will get my mission accomplished with this phone call. Constable MacLean is ingratiating and polite but I sense a kind of veiled humour behind his remarks and in the tone of his voice. He is quite enjoying all this! Perhaps I am serving to provide some comic relief from his daily routine, something for him to talk about around the office. He would not be on shift for the next couple of days, but he would speak to his Commanding Officer and get back to me himself. He concludes that, considering the circumstances, it would be better not to pass the assignment on to someone else. He will follow it through. Well, that was progress, at least. Perhaps he thinks no one would believe him if he tried to explain.

While I wait for Constable MacLean to call back, I contact the bank and explain my request to Ms. Lewinski. If the RCMP comply and actually come and get the gun, she will need written permission from me to open the box and hand it over. In addition, she will need the required two employees with her when she opens the box so that all activity can be witnessed with signatures. There is an old word my mother has often used to describe a situation that becomes complicated through unnecessary procedures – rigmarole. Getting rid of a long forgotten gun is quickly turning into a great deal of rigmarole.

I am surprised, but right after his days off, Constable MacLean phones me back. His boss emphasizes that it is an unusual request but with a copy of the will, death certificates of both Emily and Rob, and the cooperation of the bank, they will perform the necessary tasks of retrieval and disposal of the gun. I am ecstatic. Constable MacLean sounds a bit amused on the other end of the line. I cannot believe this is actually going to happen. Similar to my search for the missing man and convincing the Federal National Search Unit to include Gregory in their list of missing persons, it has been nothing but raw determination and the powers of persuasion that have proved the most useful in moving Emily's estate forward. The execution of a will is not merely what is written in that will or how others see the consequences of the content. A lot of the work involves using as much influence and creativity as possible to get the job done in an efficient and effective manner. Constable MacLean calls me after he picks up the gun, just to confirm my decision to have it destroyed.

"Have you ever been shot, Constable, either in the line of duty or otherwise?"

"No? Well I have, and the world just doesn't need another gun." Interestingly, he didn't argue.

Chapter 10
The Trappings of Life

As you have seen so far, Emily has a lot of stuff. Once we clear out the clothes, the medications, and all the papers, the house seems a more distant reflection of Emily, although the feeling of her is still around me. Crammed to the very rafters with objects that could have belonged to anyone, I still feel wrapped in the multi-textured fabric of her life every time I turn the key to unlock the door. It's as if I am prying, looking into private places, and handling her personal life without her permission. It is time to appraise everything left, including the contents of the safety deposit boxes in Alberta. I cannot do this overwhelming task alone. I need a licensed and bonded appraiser whom I trust.

I have been an auction fan most of my life. As a child, I lived with my family in a new subdivision that backed on to a hayfield where outdoor auctions were held every other Saturday, rain or shine. Not wishing to date myself, I will reveal that this took place during the time when a child of eight or nine could wander independently among the old tables, wobbly chairs, commode sets, and iron bedsteads; could reach out and touch a ragged quilt or thumb through a photo album filled with brown and grey images of frowning and stern dead relatives of someone or other. I learned to go early, so I could access the "smalls" on all the trestle tables without having to weave through potential buyers standing three deep picking through sets of dishes, cups and saucers, or collections of everything from jewellery to salt and pepper shakers. I learned to check each piece for damages. I listened to people talking and, gradually, I understood the difference between the second hand, the old, and the antique. If I looked interested enough, some kind soul would take a moment to educate me in the nuances of collecting whatever I happened to be admiring at the time.

I carefully studied all the workers at the auction. There was the auctioneer, of course. The good ones performed for the crowd like a cross between a country singer and a hog caller. The words would be loud and repetitive, with a singsong cadence and a language that only the trained ear could truly understand. There was the clerk recording each piece that sold and the number of the bidder who won the item. There was the runner who navigated the slips from the clerk at the front to the cashier at the back – an important job. If someone wanted to pay for their goods and leave, the cashier required the slips to add up their total and cash them out. Then there were the spotters. They held up the items and watched the crowd for interest, eyeballing a bidder and holding them in their gaze, yelling out a loud "yes" when that bidder's card went up, whereupon the auctioneer raised the price again. There were a number of spotters and the goods were held up for all to see, one after the other after the other, until eventually every item in the yard was christened with the hammer coming down and the magic of "sold" hanging in the air. There were always regulars at the auctions. As a child, I came to recognize the collectors, the dealers, and the idly curious. As an adult, I go to auctions and talk to someone for an extended period of time, totally familiar with what they are searching for this day but never knowing their name. We are the "auction flies". That's what we are called.

Auctioneers come from different places in life as well. Many auctioneers are also dealers of antiques, second hand goods, or used furniture. I have always preferred attending the auctions of those auctioneers that are not dealers as well. This way, the buyers are assured the best things from an estate or collection have not been skimmed off the top in order to be sold via a dealer network behind the scenes.

I need to have an auction to liquidate the remaining items in Emily's house after the personal things are removed, so I call auctioneer and appraiser Jasper Roland. I have known Jasper for many years and I like him. He is very good at his work, but can be testy on auction day. He seems to be able to work indefinitely without breaks. He has high expectations of those around him. He is very knowledgeable about a myriad of things. My decision to choose Jasper is based primarily on trust. I trust Jasper to treat me fairly and to protect Emily's privacy throughout the process. We decide to meet at Emily's on a weekend shortly after Christmas. Jasper will not have another auction until mid–March, but I need his appraisal for the court and a firm date in order to organize a possession date for the new owners of the house. As much as I love auctions and old things, I have never experienced the idea of formally appraising a complete estate. Jasper is terribly thorough. First off, we do the tour. I take him through the kitchen, laundry, and back entry area so he can see all the cooking paraphernalia, the shelves of cook books, and the bunny collection. He opens every closet door. We go through the family room and he looks at the furniture, including two beautiful reclining armchairs that are ribboned from cat claws. We look at all the dishes and crystal in the dining room as well as the oversized suite of furniture. We look at the things I have moved to the otherwise unused and empty living room. It contains some of the rug hooking supplies, the books, the dragon collection, and boxes from The Shopping Channel holding dishes that have never even been unpacked. We go upstairs to the office so he can see the collection of Chalet glass. I heave a sigh of relief when he does not head for his car after his senses are assaulted by that tacky and dusty array of ugly. We look at both bedrooms with their furniture and collectibles, including a dozen or so miniature clocks. We look at the jewellery tucked away in boxes in Emily's top dresser drawer. There are two bins of coins sitting in the family room, to which will be added the contents of the safety deposit box as yet not shipped.

The most interesting assembly of goods is in the basement, so off we head. One room contains Emily's dolls and Santas. When I say they are stacked to the ceiling, I am not exaggerating even a bit. Since Emily and Rob bought many new Barbies every year, this basement room looks like a storage facility for Toys R Us. In another room are all the trappings of Emily's parents. This includes military memorabilia, books, old clothes, and jewellery. An open area houses all the crafting materials piled high, including scroll saw books, tools, and patterns. There is a wall of plastic drawers, eight feet wide and six feet high, filled with wool for hooking. There is a sewing machine and two trunks full of fabric. There are cross stitching tools and books about every craft imaginable. There is the collection of toy trucks left to Gregory, and on top of everything, literally, the evidence of the two cats that once enjoyed this area for their litter box and as their go-to place when they were sick. The tour presents its challenges. As we walk through the house, my biggest concern is that Jasper will tell me it is too much and he's not interested. Perhaps he will just do the appraisal but not consent to do the auction. Perhaps he will do the auction but not include packing up the stuff and getting it to Halifax for the sale. Maybe he will not be able to do it all by the end of March. My stomach is in knots and my head is pounding. We have known each other a long time. Perhaps he sees the anxiety in my eyes. Perhaps he can sense my desperation. Perhaps he will simply take pity on me.

After the tour, when I think we are finished, Jasper starts his work in earnest. Every item has to be listed. Each piece of jewellery is assessed individually with some surprises along the way. In fact, Rob obviously liked his rings, as there is a fair bit of value there. In talking with Jasper as he methodically goes through the items, we discover things I see as valueless where Jasper sees worth. Some items, I assume will net the estate a generous sum, whereas Jasper doesn't see them as money makers at all. The cold January light fades as he methodically examines everything so he can return home and make a complete list and provide me with a formal appraisal. In addition, we talk about the process of collecting, packing, moving, and selling everything with the exception

of the coins and trucks which have been left to specific beneficiaries. Finally, I provide him with the itemization from
the safety deposit boxes in Alberta. These have to be included
in the appraisal as well.

Jasper agrees to conduct the auction. His people will
come and pack. They will load everything just a day or
two before the auction date to avoid storage charges. They
will need a key, if I cannot be there (and I can't, as I am
working). What will be done with the things they do not
see as fit for auction? No matter how many times one goes
through a house, there will always be garbage left behind like
the cracked flower pots, broken dust pans, glued-together
ornaments, and empty picture frames from The Dollar Store.
Jasper agrees to take all the garbage to the dump, as well - for
a fee, of course, but everything has its price. Now, you may
ask why I did not take on this job of selling Emily's things
myself. I could have an auction right on site at the house.
I could sell her collectibles on Ebay or Kijiji, following the
advice I gave her many times. I could have yard sales or a tag
sale in the house. These are all viable options and worth considering, depending on the size of the estate and the distance
you happen to be from the objects in question. I am a long
way away.

Everything, except the dining room suite, has to be out
and the house professionally cleaned before the final inspection and closing. My biggest personal advantage is that I
really trust Jasper. I know his people will come in and pack.
They will accomplish the most work possible in the shortest
amount of time. I know that nothing of value will be mistak-
enly taken to the dump and I know I will be charged fairly
for the service. Just like a politician, an executor has to have a
tight and trustworthy circle of supporters in order to get the
job done effectively and efficiently. Jasper is one of my very
limited circle, along with his staff. Violet and Henry, next
door, will let him in and will lock the door when they leave.

Once the plan is put in place, and as hard as it is for me
to believe, everything goes smoothly. Jasper returns home and
completes his appraisal. He sends me the detailed list along
with his invoice for the time he spent. The document goes

into the final probate package along with the appraisals of the house and van, and the list of all monies in accounts and due to Emily upon her death. I put all the paperwork together and send it to the lawyer where it is forwarded to the probate court and I am sent a final bill for probate taxes along with the legal bill to cover this phase of the process. There are lots of bills for the estate to pay. Hopefully, we will make a few dollars from the sale of the house contents to cover some of them. By this time, I start to feel pressure from the beneficiaries but I am confident, with the house sold, I will be able to cover the full amount of the cash bequests.

I decide not to go to the auction. Many people ask me if I intend to go and are surprised when I say no. I have fulfilled my responsibility regarding Emily's things and now it is up to Jasper and his staff to do what they do best. I do not relish the idea of wandering around in the auction hall, letting my eyes slide over the mountains of toys, letting my fingers caress the familiar fabrics or thumb through the cartons of books. Everything will just scream Emily and I have about had it. A famous family therapist named Virginia Satyr once spoke about how draining family therapy could be. She said that being a family therapist was like having a body covered in tits with people sucking on you day after day; eventually you start to feel a little wrung out. My state of mind at the time of the auction causes Virginia Satyr to pop into my head. I simply cannot stand around that hall and talk to people about Emily. I have nothing left to give. I spend the day at home cuddled up on the couch with my dog. I read a book and watch a movie. I have no recollection of the title of either.

The first time back in the house with everything gone is shockingly difficult. I am so pragmatic, I simply assume I will go in, sweep up the remnants of truck loading and packing, and that will be it. The house will be owned by someone else in a week's time and we are now only there to clean. But suddenly that empty house represents all that I have lost. It hits me like a blast of arctic air. The four months since Emily's death have been filled with her presence in everything I have done. With the house cleaned out and sold, the cold emptiness surrounds me. The hollowness of my footsteps on the hardwood floors emphasizes the echo that would forever be my friendship with Emily.

The auction nets more than I expect and the expenses are reasonable for the work that is done. Someone pays one hundred dollars for a box of rocks. As a result, my admiration for the venue, my susceptibility to auction fever, my excitement in that first step through the door to cast my eyes over all the potential treasures, has not been diminished with this particular experience from the other side of the table. If someone is willing to pay that kind of money for a box of rocks, then my childhood love of auctions, and unwavering faith in the process, lives on.

Chapter 11

The Beneficiaries

Being a beneficiary of a portion of an estate can be a troubling circumstance. On the one hand, you are advised of money or articles you will receive in the future. On the other hand, this money and these articles are administered by someone else and the process is out of your control. If you are able to avoid imagining the consequences of the resolution of the estate - what you will be doing with the money; what use you will put to the items received - then the complications of estate administration, and the passage of what always seems to be an inordinate amount of time, are less likely to be burdensome. If you start imagining yourself spending the money or using the items the minute you receive word of your inheritance, then the actual time it takes to execute the will becomes intolerable.

Emily's will includes many beneficiaries, all of whom are to receive money in one form or another and two that actually are to be given estate items. She wrote her will within a year after Rob passed away and I am executing that will some nine years later. It has never been revised. Consequences are suffered as a result.

I base my death notifications on the list of beneficiaries. Specific sums have been left to five of Rob's relatives. In addition, money and items have been left to Gregory. Money has been left in trust to the son of family friends. That family has also been left items. Finally, the remaining money is to be split between three charities with a smaller percentage going to me for my efforts. I feel the pressure to perform from the very beginning. People have been left substantial amounts of money and my biggest stressor is that I might not realize enough cash from the liquidation of the estate to pay up. As per protocol, each beneficiary is sent a letter with a copy of the sliver of the will that references their name and bequest. The lawyer puts a caveat in the letter stating they will receive this particular sum of money or an equivalent proportion if the estate does not realize the funds necessary to honour all the bequests. I get calls. Emily's beneficiaries, at least some of them, assume for whatever the reason, that Emily was loaded and therefore the estate is flush with cash and able to pay out right away. Even if that were the case, in circumstances where there is no spouse, the slowly turning wheels of probate must be endured. Those wheels are not turning fast enough to suit many. I have been told by the lawyer that I am not to discuss details of the will with any of the beneficiaries. Nevertheless, I try to explain the steps necessary for me to take in order to liquidate the estate and get them their money. There are issues. Just who the hell am I anyway? Why isn't someone from the family involved in doing this? Calls and emails go to the lawyer. Of course, the lawyer rarely answers emails or returns phone calls to the beneficiaries in question, but every contact costs the estate money, whether a response is made or not.

One particular beneficiary calls me regularly. This person is short of money, deeply in debt, and desperate for cash. I explain the process over and over. I cannot forecast how long it will take to get the accounts through Revenue Canada. I cannot tell how long it will take to sell Emily's house. Each time I hang up the phone, I am exhausted and anxious. I wish I could just send this person their cheque and be done with it, but until I am sure that everything has been settled in a way that will suit the court, my hands are tied.

There are only two actual items left to beneficiaries. These are the coin collection for the family of the child receiving the trust bequest and a set of toy trucks left to the elusive

Gregory who has yet to be located. There is no mention in the will about pictures or mementos to be distributed to family members. As executor, I have some leeway with items of sentimental value. As I go through the house, I start to put aside family pictures and items of interest, especially military, which relate to Rob and his father. In the end, I collect two huge boxes and send them off to the primary family member mentioned in the will. I find a "time capsule" tote box in the collectible room in the basement, with a note on the top saying all these things have been placed in here for the child who is inheriting the trust. I call the family and they come to pick it up. This is tricky. There are now two children and since Emily did not update her will, anything in the will and the note written on the tote are all focused on the elder child. Emily talked to me about revising her will. She wanted to take a look at it after Christmas. She died in November. I have a private discussion with the parents. We are going to treat the tote as if it is for both children. They will share the toys and it will be treated as a joint gift from Rob and Emily. The parents of these children are kind and wise. As my decision to turn over the trusteeship to them crystallizes in my mind, they continue to impress me, and I am convinced I am doing the right thing.

In the end, I make a huge executor decision regarding the child trust. At the time of writing her will, Emily left a bequest in trust for a particular child until that child turns thirty years old. At the time of Emily's death, the child is only ten, meaning I will be responsible for administering this trust until I am well into my eighties. Again, as with many portions of this will, I question the motivation of a lawyer who writes a will and suggests that this set of circumstances is acceptable. I argue that it is inappropriate for me to carry out this bequest as the resulting consequence could be that if I die before the child turns thirty, my own executor will have to take over the management of the trust. I ask about turning this task over to the parents, perfectly responsible people. There are questions. What was Emily's motivation in not setting the trust up in care of the parents in the first place? Why did I not say something to her about this when

I first read the will? I can only surmise regarding the former. The couple was young at the time and the child only a baby. Perhaps Emily felt they needed trusteeship for the money to prevent temptation. I have no such feelings and it is ten years later. They are responsible people. As to the latter question, the answer is very simply, "Beats me". Reading someone's will when they are standing beside you is, as I have said before, akin to poking in their underwear drawer while they stand in the doorway and watch. Given the chance to do it all again, I would ask more questions. It costs the estate both time and money to transfer the trusteeship for the child from myself to the parents. I feel it's the right thing to do and forge ahead to have it completed. The court process takes months.

The calls from beneficiaries who want their money are coming on a fairly regular basis. I hear from one particular relative frequently and his calls are getting desperate. I discover, later, that he calls the lawyer and expresses suspicions that I may be misusing funds and he is not going to get his money. Another relative calls a couple of times, insisting they be told "my cut". In the first place, I don't know the answer to that question and I explain, in vague terms, that I have been left a small percentage of the remainder of the estate. I expect this amount to be relatively close to standard executors' fees but tax free as Emily was kind enough to make my portion a bequest instead. This beneficiary calls the estate lawyer who repeats the same story and charges the estate for the extended amount of time he spends talking on the phone. A beneficiary engages another lawyer to communicate with the estate lawyer. More charges to the estate. No more information. This person does not express anxiety about the amount of her bequest. She is preoccupied with my role and what monies I will realize.

Another beneficiary wants to know what is going to happen with the "leftover' money", if there is any. Each beneficiary receives information regarding their bequest. This clearly documents their place in the will. No one is privy to the whole will except the court, and those institutions and businesses that need proof of death and executorship. I explain that the residual amount in the estate, after all the bills are paid and the bequests are forwarded, will belong to three separate charities with a smaller portion going to me for my efforts. It never ends.

Finally, after the house is sold and the auction is completed, after all the bills are paid for the estate, after all the insurances have been deposited, the lawyer finally allows me to distribute the cash allotments to the five initial beneficiaries and deliver the coins to the family who inherited them. I cannot do any of this before we are absolutely sure there is money remaining for the child's trust and for the missing person's bequest.

Every beneficiary is to sign a release when receiving their money or item. In the case of the five, I make out the cheques and include the release letter to be signed, witnessed, and returned. I include a stamped, self-addressed envelope along with a copy of their reference portion of the will. Each letter is registered, so I can track receipt and see a copy of the signature on line. I, like the lawyer, am nervous that one or more of the five may not respect the process. The court will want proof that all the monies were distributed in accordance with the will. It would be great to get back all the release letters signed and dated. In the end, we do, and I am immensely grateful to be one step closer to the finish. I only hear from one of the beneficiaries again, in the form of a very thoughtful thank-you card. The others, including the person who was so intent on getting his money as soon as possible, finally returns his signed release letter and that is the end of that.

The delivery of the coins is a much more rewarding experience. After all this time, I desperately search for anything positive to gain from the whole ordeal of executing a will. There are a lot of coins. The overloaded plastic storage bins and framed collections, along with the boxes from Alberta, fill the back of our little Toyota Matrix. The family has no idea of the volume of coins or about the challenges we had to retrieve a large portion of them from out west. We travel to Elmsville loaded down. They wait for us and we open the car to expressions of both shock and awe. It's great. I smile, remembering their reactions. The coins are lugged into the house and the requisite release form is signed. I have included books about coin collecting we found stashed away with the coin inventory. The family is overwhelmed and we spend an hour with them to reminisce about Rob and Emily, shedding a few tears and laughing about our mutual experiences. We have a private chat about the trust and the steps necessary to make it their responsibility instead of mine. They are patient, pleasant, and cooperative. It will all work out in the end. They know the process is well under way.

Besides Gregory's bequests, there are the three charities left the residual of Emily's estate. They do not get their money at the same time as the original five. Everything must go through Probate Court a final time before the child's trust, the missing man's trust, and the charities can be paid out, but since I am discussing beneficiaries with you, I will tell you about this portion of the process now. In reading the will initially, and I have to admit, almost until the time of final disbursements, I assume the charities are: a women's shelter chosen by me, the Pet Care Society, and the local food bank. In actual fact, upon closer scrutiny, the first was correct, but the Pet Care Society is in an area of the province not local to Emily's home, and the food bank is not the local food bank for which Emily had worked so hard, but another group that was in existence in another county prior to the creation of the local food bank and prior to Emily's involvement. I can't explain any of this. I can't tell you if Emily did not properly proof read her will and the address for a Pet Care Society branch outside her community passed inspection without notice. I can tell you that Emily's will was not updated in the nine years since its creation and much had changed in her life in those nine years. She made it clear to me prior to her death, her intentions of updating her will in the New Year. Of course, this does not happen. As a result, I am left sending a substantial amount of money to the Pet Care Society outside her community, as well as delivering the same amount of money to an organization not even associated with the local food bank to which she had devoted so much of her time.

Do I take all this business a bit personally? Why, yes, as a matter of fact, I do. The charities receive the monies they do because of my work in liquidating the estate in as cost efficient and budget conscious a manner as possible. The original five get all the money bequeathed to them for the same reasons. If I had decided initially to turn the administration of this estate over to the lawyers, I fully expect beneficiaries to be still waiting and I am sure the monies realized would only be a portion of those received as everything would be constantly chewed up in legal fees. I mean no disrespect. That is just the way it is. I am amazed at how much money it costs, even with all the work I managed to do myself. My pleasure comes from sending out those cheques for the full amount and from knowing, through feedback from a few, how much it is appreciated.

Chapter 12

The Beach

The human body, when cremated, creates a considerable amount of ash. Of course, exact amounts were never part of my life experience until my visit with the funeral director to pick up the ashes of both Emily and Rob. Rob's ashes sat in a square marble urn on Emily's dresser for ten years. There was a brass plaque on the side of the box with an engraved likeness of Rob. I remember, at the time of Rob's death, this memorial to him being so incredibly important to Emily. My husband lugged it down to the funeral home after Emily's house was sold, to store it in a safe place, along with Emily's ashes, until we could carry out her wishes as described in the will.

Cooper, the sweet young man who possesses that typical quiet voice so necessary in the funeral business, pairs his professionalism with his perfectly atypical sense of humour and prepares for me to pick up the ashes of both Emily and Rob that summer following her death. We worked together so well when Emily died, that formality is no longer a necessity when we speak. "Bring a couple of good sized buckets," he suggests. "There will be a lot of ashes." We load the car with two white plastic gyproc mud buckets. They are one and a half kilogram pails, to be exact, with very sturdy lids. Cooper quickly whisks them away after I arrive at the funeral home with the empties. He returns with the two, lids secure, and

101

presents me with a small vial in addition. "This will be for when you find her mother's grave," he says with a smile. "If the wind is blowing really hard, you don't want to open those bucket lids unless you really mean it. The ash is light, but there's a lot of it and it'll blow everywhere. Do I have to tell you to check the wind first?" Now he is grinning.

Poor Emily, I thought. You're making your last trip in a plastic pail.

At the very first opportunity, David and I take Emily and Rob to the beach. She requested their ashes be scattered on a south shore beach and I choose the one across the bay from our home, where I can see the waves crashing every day. There are some criteria that have to be met for us to perform this ultimate task. The night has to be calm, for obvious reasons, and such opportunities are few and far between on this edge of the Atlantic. The tide has to be out and the beach as unoccupied as possible. We leave the house just shortly after eight o'clock on the most beautiful August evening. It is not quite dusk and the sky has that magical mix of daytime azure and evening indigo. The skies in this part of the world, particularly at this time of the year, seem to wrap around you like a cloak. We drive to the edge of the dunes, park the car, and carry the two buckets across the boardwalk and down to the beach. The tide is moving out. The wet sand is packed like concrete under my bare feet. My footprints are deeper than usual, carrying Emily's ashes with the metal wire handle digging into my palm. The smell of the tide pools, filled with periwinkles, seaweed, ownerless shells, and the ecosystems of frail sea life leave a salty whisper on my cheeks and lips, comforting me with its familiarity. I smile to myself, burdened with all this emotion and still looking like just another quahog digger taking advantage of a receding tide on a balmy summer night.

There are too many people on the beach. Now, as I understand it in this province, there are no hard and fast laws about scattering or not scattering ashes, but somehow I feel that privacy and the cover of darkness need to be in our favour. As we sit side by side on a rock, staring out at the water, listening to the distant rumbling and rippling as the waves became smaller and further away, we talk about Emily and Rob. Perhaps we talk *to* Emily and Rob. "Do you see what we are doing? Do you have any idea how hard this is? I hope you are happy with my decisions." The sun is setting and the beach wanderers are starting to head for the paths and back to their cars. The tide is far out now and the breaking waves, unaffected by the late summer breeze, are remote and hushed in the quiet of the evening air. My feet are cold and we haven't even really hit the water yet. We stand up, look around to ensure our privacy, and start to walk out between two rock formations toward those distant waves. My bare feet seek the safety of flat compacted spaces tucked between the rocks embedded in the sand. Eventually, I have to balance rock to rock, making my way further and further from shore. We go as far as we can go, to the water's edge at low tide, and then wade in to scatter their ashes. This is what we do, quietly, side by side, in the soft purple of an August night, bent low to the water, scattering, mixing, and moving as ghosts ourselves.

It takes almost an hour to scatter the ashes from both buckets and navigate back to the beach, across the rocks and through the pools. Hand in hand we head to the car, down the road, and return to the comfort of home.

No one knows exactly where Emily and Rob's ashes were spread. Emily wanted no one to know. She trusted me to follow her wishes and not to ask anyone else to share the experience. I understand there are those who might feel left out, who might even feel robbed of an opportunity to go to a special place to remember. I relate to their emotion. I was so overwhelmed when I found Emily's family plot in little Charles River the month before. Then again, I was given a task and my job was to execute that task.

The next morning, I stand on my deck overlooking the bay, wrapped in the same morning sunshine as the waves that lap around my friends and twinkle in the distance. The comforting aroma of hazelnut coffee drifts up from a mug whose shape has been memorized by my hands, and I know in that moment that we did the best we could to honour Emily's wishes. It was tough – one of the hardest things I have ever done. The soft, salt breeze brushes my cheeks as the tide quietly rolls in, spreading across the rocks with gurgling murmurs of good morning.

Chapter 13
Not Quite Done Yet

In a perfect world, this whole ordeal of executorship would be over by now, but it soon becomes clear there is still more work in store for me.

It is now August and Emily has been dead for more than nine months. During that time, her two chubby, spoiled and geriatric felines are moved to a perpetual shelter and subsequently adopted by a single lady who cannot resist their beguiling charms. Her funeral is held in her home community and her ashes scattered as instructed in her will. Her van is cleaned and sold to a lovely family from the other side of the province. Her life's possessions are sorted, recycled, given to charity, or appraised and auctioned. An estate account is established, her taxes are paid, insurances collected, mortgage paid out and investments collapsed. The contents of her safety deposit boxes in Alberta are assessed, appraised, shipped, and sorted. The gun is destroyed. The five primary beneficiaries are paid in full and the coin collection bequest is safely delivered.

I have cried and stressed over Emily's pathetic old cats. Funeral arrangements were made where no instructions existed, which resulted in both accolades and criticism. Her ashes were disposed of privately and in secret, much to the chagrin of those who expected me to make exceptions to the will stipulating the ritual be private. I experienced both sadness and wonder at the state of her vehicle. Shock, grief, and overwhelming exhaustion wrapped me in a blanket of what could have become hopelessness as I clawed my way through the process of dealing with all her possessions. I stressed over selling the house and felt my hackles rise as the buyers tried, initially, to take advantage of the untenable situation in which they knew I found myself. The kindness and caring of many balanced my suffering through the impatience and anger of a few. I obsessed about the gun. Emily was channelled on more than one occasion, in attempts to locate objects and understand the mysteries of her logic. I talked to hundreds and hundreds of people throughout this initial nine months, learning much more than it is possible to evaluate and report.

When the clearance certificate finally arrives from Revenue Canada in early November, I go ahead and schedule an appointment with the estate lawyer in Albertville. I want to have a face to face discussion about the final process to get through probate, establish the child's trust, detail the missing man's trust with the Public Trustee, and distribute the last of the funds to the charities. Shortly before this meeting is to take place, I start getting sick. First, my voice gets gravelly and I am short of breath. People remark on how weird I sound. I visit my doctor who thinks I have a bit of a viral infection in my throat and that perhaps I need to stay home for a few days. Up to this point in my working life, I have never taken more than two sick days in a row and I currently have not called in sick in eight years. This can't be happening. There is simply no time to be sick. I stay home for a couple of days, take a third day to be sure, and then use my scheduled biweekly day off to go to Albertville to the appointment already set up with the lawyer.

My husband thinks it best if he drives as my condition seems to be getting worse rather than better. Considering I am using all the strength I can muster just to hold my head up, he is likely quite wise. The walk from the car, down the blustery street and into the little vestibule of the law office with its stale air and uncomfortable chairs, is about all I can manage. Sitting in the waiting room, hunched over like an old lady, wrapped in my winter squall coat, concentrating completely on my attempts to propel air in and out of my lungs without dissolving into fits of coughing, I can feel myself deteriorating further still. Coughing is the worst. The pain is so extreme it feels like my ribs must be broken. The lawyer takes forever to come downstairs and as he crosses the oriental carpet of the reception room floor, all dapper and crisp like an ad for Brooks Brothers, smiling that political hand shaking grin, he looks at me and says, "You look awful. Come on in." I tell him I have a virus and will not shake hands. He asks me which door knobs I have touched so he can avoid them.

The meeting is short. It has nothing to do with writing cheques and distributing the final assets. It has to do with the process of preparing the "Executor's Account". He explains, and slowly because it appears he thinks that sick people are also demented, his office has to present these accounts to Probate Court and it has forty-five days to review them for errors, omissions, or problems of one sort or another. My package of information regarding my search for Gregory has already been forwarded to him and I am surprised that it still has to go to court. The whole issue about the accounts is total news to me. At no time, during this lengthy process, have I been told that my ledger would have to go to court in some form or another. He tells me I can't do this myself. It must be done by his assistant, Terry Stilling. With the originals of all the receipts for the entire estate, the appraisals, the ledger, and all the bank statements, she will complete the Executor's Account based on a form and formula as set out by the court. I will need to forward every original document to the office before she can get started. And, I might want to keep copies of everything just in case they lose something. And, yes, every detail is required including receipts for miscellaneous stamps and envelopes. My book work for the estate is in pretty good shape. I have kept track of office expenses and travel, for which we have reimbursed ourselves along the way. My file folders are organized and I will be able to put my hands on everything required but I am too sick to appreciate the work already completed. For whatever the reason, and likely through my viral fog, all I can think about is the mountain of photocopying that will need to be done. He also tells me to take my time over Christmas. No point in sending all that stuff to Albertville right before the holiday. Now, perhaps I should just get out of his office and quit contaminating the world in general. I need to go home and go to bed, right? Lawyer's orders. No handshake, of course. Merry Christmas.

Within a week, I am diagnosed with pneumonia and it gets a lot worse before it gets better. It's Christmas Day before I turn that elusive corner of improvement. I have been badly hurt before, as you already know, but have never been this sick. Coping is a major challenge. I feel as if I need to accomplish something every day and some days I can do no more than stretch out in a chair in front of the television. I discover there is actually room in a person's life for watching paint dry. I see a lot of Home and Garden Television. It is five weeks before I am able to go back to work. During this time, I focus bit by bit on those accounts, insuring every entry in the ledger has its accompanying documentation, assembling the various appraisals, and sorting all the bank statements from the original accounts and investments through to the present estate account.

In early January, with copies made, the originals of all my precious accounts are couriered to the charming and helpful Terry Stilling. She calls me immediately after she receives them, to compliment me on my organization, and go through some of the details. Terry, I am delighted to discover, is a lot like myself. She likes to be organized and she is a communicator, unlike her boss. She goes over the process with me, so that I have an idea of what lies ahead.

With Terry, the final details of the Executor's Account, the child's trust, the missing beneficiary, and those godforsaken toy trucks all get processed. My accounts are approved on June 15, 2011 - one year, seven months, and two days after Emily's death. Apparently, this is quick but I am hard to convince. We meet one last time to sign the final cheques.

There is an old expression and it goes something like this: When you are up to your ass in alligators, it's tough to remember your intention was to drain the swamp. For the first year following the death of my friend, I am so embroiled in the process of executing her will, that I find it difficult to remember what life was like before this myriad of tasks confronted me. I have, what I assume, is lots of relevant experience, having run my own business, written a Masters thesis, planned projects for the government, and built a couple of houses. I see myself as a natural planner, organizer, and more than a bit anal when it comes to the details. My maternal grandmother was a consummate list maker. My father was a meticulous accountant. I come by my attributes quite honestly, in my opinion. My life and work experiences, coupled with my practicality, are all I need to get the job done, right? Sure, all the little bits and pieces help. Nevertheless, the realization of how utterly unprepared I am for the tasks at hand comes almost immediately.

One might logically assume that to engage the law firm where Emily originally obtained her will would smooth out the edges and expedite the process. This is not the case for me and is likely not the norm for anyone. The firm does not facilitate the execution of this will any quicker or with more expertise than any other law firm and given a "do over", I would take the whole kit and caboodle to my own solicitor. At least I would be in the company of someone I already know and where an open relationship is already established. Not knowing what is going on is bad for me. Not being able to anticipate consequences and next moves is also bad. My best work happens when I understand the process and am able to plan my actions based on what lies ahead, as well as what is happening in the here and now.

It comes as a surprise to realize that every decision about Emily's estate rests solely on my shoulders. Initially, this is overwhelming. During discussion, with any of the parties or within my circle of trusted people, I hear the phrase, "it is your decision", more times than I can count. Eventually, I lose hope that anyone will make a decision independent of me, and of course, they never will. From whether or not to throw out an old cookie sheet or send it to auction, to whether or not to repair the garburator, it all ends up in my lap. I develop a real skill for making decisions and moving along. There is no time to revisit or second-guess myself. There is just too much to do.

I develop an ongoing agitation regarding the loss of control over my time. As a professional with a regular full-time job, I live by my agenda. Meetings are booked weeks in advance. There is a requirement to be certain places at certain times to complete certain tasks for my work. Everything is always laid out with others having access to my where-abouts during the work day. So, to drop everything and run to Albertville, a two hour trip, and sign a few forms, is not an option. My weekends end up being planned with the detail and precision of a complicated advance on a battlefield. All bets are off if an unanticipated task materializes out of nowhere. Everything changes in the blink of an eye.

I manage as best I can throughout the process by organizing and reorganizing; by keeping meticulous notes I do not know will be needed until much later; by maintaining detailed records of transactions I do not know will be sent to court until further along in the process; by creating a very close-knit group of friends and advisers around me; and by remembering, at the front of my mind at all times, Emily and my understanding of her wishes, struggling to do the best I can for her under terribly trying circumstances. Never losing sight of the value of this process, I still keep an envelope of pictures, the birth announcement and a letter from his birth father for Gregory, in case he ever calls.

I learn a lot about my friends Emily and Rob after their deaths. There is a team building social work game about self-analysis which involves a person trying to compare how they see themselves with how others see them. This can be quite revealing in a workshop with twenty people all using bits of paper to write hastily compiled remarks about the kind of person they are, based on how they have presented during the course of your interactions with them. Many times, your idea of how you see yourself has little or nothing to do with how others see you. How I saw the Maxwells as a couple and individually before their deaths, and how I came to see them afterwards, prove to be quite different indeed. My adventure through their home, their history, and their belongings gave me a much better idea of how they likely saw themselves. I often wonder how they would feel if they knew what I know now.

Emily and Rob were deeply in love. Throughout their lives together, they overlooked each other's weaknesses. Rob loved Emily regardless of her endless struggles with her weight. Emily supported Rob's dreams for the future no matter how totally unrealistic. They planned for a life that would never be. The whole time I knew them as a couple, they pined for a home by the ocean with water access, a boat, and a big sun porch overlooking the sea. This would never have happened and I see that clearly now. They did not have, and would never have had, the funds for such a venture. In the unique relationship of Emily and Rob, it was the dream that became important, not the realization. They were never that practical. When not dreaming of the future, they were living in the past. Things had been better back when they were in the service. Very little of their life together was grounded in the present, or in reality, I came to discover. They always expected those toys they bought at Zellers every year after Christmas to increase in value and become tomorrow's collectibles. If they were alive today, they would still be waiting. They always thought The Inn would sell for hundreds of thousands of dollars when they eventually decided to retire and we know what happened there. Each of them, unknown to the other, denied the gravity of Rob's illness in the hope of protecting each other from the reality and pain of his eventual demise. They both thought they were experts at just about anything you could imagine. They refused to acknowledge their weaknesses and alienated anyone who might see fit to argue a point. They were generous and giving to those about whom they cared the most, but they could not remotely tolerate those they disliked. You were either friend or foe. There was never much grey area for Emily and Rob.

As in her life with Rob, Emily seemed to spend much of her time wandering in her fantasy world of good health, good diet, lots of pretty clothes, a dream house with her husband, and regular entertaining. In reality, she was gradually losing control of both her health and her weight. Her money was running out. Her home was filled with items of the past, from which she could not part. She put on a brave face for her charities and hooking guild, but eventually could not even manage the day-to-day responsibilities of running a home and taking care of her cats. Her real world and her fantasy life never collided until her death. Is it what we leave behind that tells the story of who we really were?

I change as a result of managing Emily's estate. For one thing, I pay closer attention to what I keep in the drawer of my bedside table. I call my mother and tell her that if she has anything in her house she doesn't want me to see, to get rid of it now. Lasting impressions are made in what you leave behind. I do not want anyone lifting up a corner of the carpet of my life and finding all the dirty bits I never took the time to resolve. Finish business. Clear the decks. We are all on the same path. After writing the final cheques and returning home, I clean house. I throw out anything not needed and have a big yard sale besides. Although I have never been much of an accumulator and am a minimalist by nature, I have become quite mercenary about this whole aspect of my life now. My poor mother eventually suffers the consequences. She has recently moved from her home of sixty years to an apartment. We downsize to the point where my mother, the consummate collector of all things beautiful, thinks she is not even going to be permitted to have a Nippon bowl on the dining room table or the mantle clock on the sideboard. We laugh for three days as we go through her house, me on the step ladder, her sitting at the table. I reach in the cupboard and pull out one of the dozens of cups and saucers. Does she keep it? Will it be given to someone? Is it to be sent to auction? We do this hundreds and hundreds of times. Every item has a story and I finally tell my eighty-eight year old mother, who is going through one of the most traumatic experiences of her life, that she may only tell one story for every five things or we will be at this for a month and we only have three days. Six months later, she still calls and asks me if such and such got moved, given away, or sold. We never fail to have a giggle over the whole process. I could not have been convinced, prior to her deciding to sell her home, that we would ever be able to joke about the disposition of her life's possessions. In the end, it is just stuff.

I learn something else from Emily. I do not like the discovery of this different person behind closed doors. I feel a little cheated, if the truth be known. I thought we were friends and close enough to be honest and really know each other, warts and all. I was wrong. The result, for me, is I have stopped pretending even a little in my own relationships. I always thought I needed to try a little harder; be the person others wanted me to be or they would not like me. No more of that. I am who I am and to coin a phrase – "what you see is what you get". Through all this, I become quite disillusioned with the politically correct dancing required of me at my place of work and I subsequently retire. I do what I want to do now, with people of my own choosing. What a liberating feeling.

Since Emily's death, I have updated my will, made a contact list for my executor, straightened out my file cabinet (yet again) and completed revised medical directives. I have talked all this over with my executor and supported both my husband and my mother in going through the same process.

Emily is in my thoughts every day and often. Reminders of her are peppered throughout my house in the form of gifts she gave me over the years. For a long time, I was cross with her. She really left me in a horrible predicament and with an incredible amount of work. I wondered if she knew how difficult all this would be and did not care. I wanted to take the pewter framed hummingbird down off my kitchen wall, give the shell chimes away, and try to forget her altogether. Time changes all that. I am not the same person I was before Emily died. The loss of her friendship and the management of her estate have changed the way I view the world in general and my life in particular. Now that it's over, I am finally able to be grateful for the experience.

Epilogue

It is impossible for me to finish my story without providing you with some tips and observations. My mother taught me it is better to share information than to keep knowledge to oneself. I have learned over the years that not everyone appreciates that quality, so you certainly do not have to partake if you don't want to do so. Also, it is my opinion alone and not from a lawyer, probate judge, or other party, legal or otherwise. It is merely me attempting to share those things my friend Emily has helped me learn on our journey together after her sudden death.

There are two parts to this whole event. The first is the actual will and how it is constructed. Everyone needs a will. The second part is about the role of executor. At some point in your life, you may well be asked to act in this capacity for a friend, a relative with no children, or a parent. You may be a co-executor and share the responsibilities with another person. Regardless of how little it is discussed, executing a will is not an uncommon role.

About Your Will:

- Make a will. It does not matter if you do not have a lot of money or stuff. Whatever you have is yours. Update it regularly, at least every 3-5 years. Life changes. You have to keep up.
- Choose your executor carefully and don't make burdensome requests of your executor. Care about them, in the sense of appreciating what they have agreed to do for you. Make their role as streamlined as possible.
- Talk to your executor about your will. Go through it with them and clarify anything that may be a bit unusual to someone else.
- Be careful about leaving chunks of money to people in your will. There may not be sufficient funds to pay them their bequest by the time you die. Think about using percentages instead.
- Ensure your beneficiaries are adequately identified with names, phone numbers and even email addresses. Keep this information updated.
- As you age, tidy your affairs periodically. Divest yourself of that attic or garage full of stuff.
- Feel free to give stuff away before you die rather than leaving disbursements to your executor.
- Keep an up-to-date list for your executor. It needs to include: names and contact information for notifications, bank account locations, safety deposit key location, insurance information, and location of all paperwork in your home.
- Make your executor a beneficiary with a percentage of the residue of the estate as an option instead of collecting standard executor fees. The former is not taxable whereas the latter is.

About Being an Executor:

- Think very carefully before consenting to be an executor.
- Ask lots of questions, regardless of how uncomfortable you might feel.
- Once the person has died, take both control and responsibility as soon as possible.
- Do not assume the law firm engaged by the deceased is necessarily the one to engage to assist with execution of the will. It may be better to go with whom you know.
- Document everything, even small details. In a year, you will never remember those details.
- Be very organized or get organized. Remember, if there is no spouse surviving and everything must go to Probate Court, all of your actions, decisions and administrations will be scrutinized by the court. The deceased belongings are not yours, but you are responsible for them.
- Gather a few trustworthy people around you to assist with tasks. The reality is that you cannot do it alone and turning the process over to someone else is not what you agreed to when you said you would be an executor.
- Create as few estate bank accounts as possible in order to keep management streamlined.
- If named as a co-executor, ensure you have a clear understanding of the kind of working relationship you will have with the other person by talking to them about the process.
- Try not to take things too personally. Keep everything at arm's length, as best as you can.
- Keep your emotions tucked away in a safe place. It is important to be able to work with lawyers, accountants, bankers, and the like without breaking down. Protect yourself by showing your feelings only when you feel safe enough to do so.

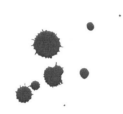

About the Author

L. P. Suzanne Atkinson was born in New Brunswick, Canada and lived in both Alberta and Quebec before settling in Nova Scotia in 1991. She has a BA in Psychology from Mount Allison University, a Bachelor of Social Work from McGill University, and an MA in Sociology from Acadia University. Suzanne spent her professional career in the fields of mental health and home care as both a therapist and trainer. She also owned and operated, with her husband, both an antique business and a construction business for more than twenty-five years.

Her philosophy of life is based on two qualities for which she continually strives. They are her benchmarks. First: there is no better descriptor than to be called a kind person and good friend. Second: a lesson learned and not shared is information squandered.

Suzanne writes about the challenges inherent in aging and about the unavoidable consequences of relationships. She uses her life and work experiences to weave timeless stories that cross many boundaries. She and her husband, David Weintraub, continue to make Nova Scotia their home.

Printed in Canada